All the Broken Bodies—

My Life as a Physical Therapist

By Martha Thomas, PT

Table of Contents

PART I   Girls Need Not Apply

PART II   Back to Belleville

PART III   Hotter Than Hell, but Healing in Phoenix

PART IV   If it's Physical, it's Therapy: Across Visible and Invisible Borders

This book is dedicated in loving memory to Jack Wing, PT.

***

This book is also written with gratitude to my late mother Maxine Thomas for believing in me, and my late grandmother Ada Boesch who was the inspiration for me choosing physical therapy as my career.

***

With heartfelt appreciation for my talented editor, Jennifer Garrity. She made my stories come to life and her encouragement and skill made this book possible.

PART I

Girls Need Not Apply

The purpose of human life is to serve, and to show compassion

and the will to help others.

—Dr. Albert Schweitzer

Introduction

A tall, raw-boned woman and a bit on the heavy side, Grandma Ada went down hard when she fell. An old knee injury made her unsteady on her feet; she used a cane to get around, but for some reason that day, she'd left it sitting unused while she made her way into the living room. The nylon stockings she wore slid right out from under her on our hardwood floor, and Grandma landed with a loud *thud*. I rushed to help her, along with my mother and brother.

Grandma burst into tears. The force of the fall had caused her to urinate on herself. Her dignity in tatters, she felt ashamed and embarrassed, so we kids pretended we didn't notice her wet clothing as we helped our mother get her into a chair. Mom took over and cleaned her up.

I adored Grandma Ada. She was pillowy soft and so kind and loving. During the fifteen years she'd lived with us on and off, she taught me how to bake delicious sweets and stitch things by hand, and she'd often shared the story of how as a child, she had fallen on an exposed railroad spike while walking train tracks with her brothers, looking for wild game in the Missouri Ozarks. Good medical care was hard to come by in her rural community, so the wound wasn't treated properly. It didn't kill her, neither did it heal correctly. She'd developed severe osteoarthritis in her knee that worsened as she aged, and now she had reinjured it, right in the comfort of our living room.

I felt so sad for Grandma Ada, and wished I could ease her pain. She'd suffered a great indignity in front of us all but thank God we were there to help her. She eventually got cortisone shots in her bad knee, but those only gave temporary relief. She lived on Bufferin and used a heating pad. As a teenager, with my newly acquired driver's license, I drove her to physical therapy appointments at Belleville Memorial Hospital, where I accompanied her to the basement. In those days, physical therapy was often relegated to basements as it was not considered an integral part of patient care.

While therapists worked with my grandmother, I waited patiently, observing all that went on around me. The PT staff were kind and helpful; they cared for my grandmother with a gentle touch, using heat, massage, and exercises to strengthen her knee. To me, it looked as if they loved their work. They seemed to be having fun and actually enjoying themselves.

I grew up in an era when girls aspired to only a handful of career options. In grade school, most of us girls had the impression that we could choose from only a handful of careers—housewife, nurse, teacher, or secretary. By the time I graduated high school, however, more young women had begun to attend college, although their career choices were still quite traditional. Most of my female friends planned to become teachers. A few chose nursing. Some wanted to go to secretarial school to hone their typing and shorthand skills. None of those career paths held any interest for me.

Times were turbulent in my graduation year of 1968. The Vietnam War was in full swing, and the violent protests it generated, as well as the assassinations of Robert Kennedy and Martin Luther King, Jr. left many of us young people feeling afraid of the future. The draft was in effect, and we lost classmates in the war. The road ahead seemed so uncertain.

I longed to move forward in life in a way that made sense in a chaotic world. I wanted to make a difference. As I watched the compassionate physical therapists do their best to ease my grandmother's suffering, it occurred to me that maybe I had found my path forward in life. If I could learn to help people deal with and recover from physical disabilities, I would make my Grandma Ada proud and enjoy a fulfilling, meaningful career.

One day, a friend and I visited the physical therapy departments in Belleville's two hospitals. At Belleville Memorial, the same facility to which I'd taken my grandmother for her appointments, we spoke to Don, the department head. Enthusiastically we told him we wanted to become therapists. To our shock and dismay, he discouraged us. "There are already too many women in the field," he said dismissively. "We need more men, not women. Why don't you girls go into nursing instead?"

That infuriated me. I knew right then and there that I would defy Don and pursue physical therapy with all I had. Before long, I was accepted to the PT program at the University of Kentucky, one of just sixteen students chosen out of around 600 applicants, and I began my studies there in 1970.

Things got off to a rough start. When confronted with the anatomy lab, I almost quit the program immediately. The stench of dead bodies mingled with formaldehyde made me physically ill. Every single day, Bob, the lab assistant, munched on donuts and sipped coffee as if the disgusting odors had no effect on him. Just watching him enjoy his snacks, even as he demonstrated how to dissect fatty tissue away from muscle and ligament attachments, made me retch. I lost my appetite. Ten pounds dropped off me during that first semester. No matter how vigorously I tried, I could not wash the sickeningly sour-sweet smell off my skin, hair, or clothing.

Thankfully, I managed to stick it out. I am so glad I did! Never have I wanted to be, or do, anything else but a physical therapist. All throughout my career, it has been immensely gratifying to assist injured people and help them become their best physical selves. Always challenging, never dull, continually rewarding, physical therapy gave back to me more than I could possibly give. I never stopped learning about how best to meet the needs of the patients who came into my care. The lessons I learned as a "body mechanic" have shaped me into the person I am today and taught me invaluable truths about life, people, and the common threads that bind us all together.

Chapter One

From Katz's to Kysoc

The inner workings of the human body have always fascinated me. As a little girl, I quickly outgrew playing with dolls in favor of playing sports with my brothers. I was on a girls' softball team. I climbed trees, roller-skated, and spent most of my summers at the local pool and swimming with the Dorchester swim team. When I wanted to do something by myself, I enjoyed tinkering around with a chemistry set and my "invisible" man and woman—plastic, see-through human forms that revealed all the bones and organs inside. Perhaps my love of sports fueled my interest in such things. Yet deep down inside, I knew I wanted to have an occupation where I could have a chance to make a difference in people's lives.

Could that have been because I'd grown up in an unstable family due to my father's alcoholism? The seeds of my tendency toward caretaking were likely sown in childhood. My parents were unhappy. Constantly worried about them, feeling sad for them, I did whatever I could to help them in ways beyond the scope of a young person's knowledge and experience. On many a morning, I tried to help my father sober up so he could go to work. I did laundry and other household chores beyond my capacity in hopes of smoothing things over and making life easier for my mother.

Grandma Ada also needed my help as I grew into my teen years. Since Mom and Dad worked full time, I drove my grandmother around town, taking her shopping and to her medical appointments. Sliding into that caregiving role felt natural to me. However, whenever the tension in our home threatened to boil over, I knew I had to take care of myself and get out of there. Many a peaceful evening was spent at friends' homes, in which alcohol played a minor or non-existent role.

My mother encouraged me to aim for college and escape the confines of our unhappy home. She wanted me to have an education and a good career, and although she realized the unhealthy environment of our household wasn't good for me, it was probably painful for her to think about letting me go. I'd been her helper for many years; I ran interference between her and Dad and tried to pick up the pieces after explosive arguments by doing practical chores my mother was in no condition to tackle. Still, she insisted on college for me, in an era when many girls considered high school graduation to be the end of their formal education.

I almost blew it! Not taking my high school studies seriously, I preferred to throw my energies into sports and social life. I'd always been somewhat of a tomboy growing up. I enjoyed being with my friends and plunged myself into the middle of every activity and event. I taught swimming lessons and relished performing in school plays.

Over time, and without fully realizing what was happening, I drifted into the role of an average student. Then one day, I had an epiphany. My part-time job at Katz's Department Store in downtown Belleville had me working in the women's wear department with several older ladies in their fifties and sixties. They hobbled around all day wearing high heels, their knees hurting, folding clothes, and ringing up purchases. One day, I stood there at the cash register, watching them. It dawned on me that this could be my future if I didn't buckle down and pay attention to my studies. Did I really want to be walking around on sore feet, doing the mindless work of folding blouses and pants for decades to come?

Absolutely not! Shaken at the prospect, I vowed to apply myself from that day forward. At sixteen and nearing the end of my junior year, I'd let a lot of water flow under the bridge. Now, I was determined to make up for lost time. I worked hard, brought my grades up, and applied for community college.

I'd already decided on physical therapy, and as I pursued the science courses I needed at Southwestern Illinois College, I blossomed academically. I hired a tutor to help me get up to speed in math, physics, and chemistry. I worked my behind off to earn top grades so I could get into the University of Kentucky's heavily science-based physical therapy program. The thought of learning more about the human body thrilled me, for by this time, I was enamored with the idea of becoming a healer.

When the acceptance letter came in the mail, I screamed, jumped up and down, and ran to show it to my parents. All that summer, I basked in a job well done. My essay on how Grandma Ada's predicament influenced me to help people suffering from physical pain must have helped sway the admissions committee, as well as the fact that I'd been blessed with glowing references.

Before I could show up for school, however, the University of Kentucky required me to give a week of my time to Camp Kysoc, a summer camp for handicapped children. In this, I was not alone; all of the university's new PT students had to report to the camp during that August of 1970. Set in a beautiful countryside property and operated by the Easter Seals Society, Camp Kysoc hosted 27,000 disabled children and adults in overnight programs from 1960 to 2010.

My week at Camp Kysoc launched me from the frying pan of academic rigor into the fire of reality. My fellow PT students and I survived only because we were young and idealistic. What an eye-opening experience to live in a cabin, surrounded by handicapped children from ages five to eighteen! All of them were in various stages of disability. Some couldn't speak. Some couldn't walk. Some had to be fed, and some were in diapers, needing to be toileted and bathed.

Mr. MacDougal, the director of the physical therapy program at the University of Kentucky, was adamant about giving us a well-rounded PT education. He wanted us to arrive with a little experience under our belts, and putting naïve, idealistic twenty-year-olds into cabins with handicapped children did the trick nicely. Nothing in my life had prepared me for that week at camp. It overwhelmed me completely!

Many of the children at Camp Kysoc had cerebral palsy. They were intelligent, with normally functioning brains, but with bodies that didn't work. Some could ambulate with jerky movements, while others were wheelchair-bound. A few of the campers had Down's syndrome. Thankfully, we weren't expected to care for them alone, but were each paired with a senior counselor who could instruct and guide us in meeting the children's needs:

"Watch carefully, Martha. This is how you get Suzy in and out of bed."

"Johnny can't feed himself. Watch how I do this; he'll look you in the eye when he's ready for another bite."

"Stephen can't speak, but he'll tilt his head a certain way when he has to go to the toilet. This is how you transfer him from his wheelchair to the commode."

It was up to me to pay close attention and put it all into practice. That week became baptism by fire for a girl who

15

dreamed of a heroic career helping the hurting. There I was—tall, slim, athletic, and healthy—confronted with the stark reality of people living with serious handicaps. Would I have the fortitude to deal with conditions like these throughout a long career of physical therapy? I couldn't imagine how parents and other caregivers managed to handle the needs of these children day in and day out, and I felt great admiration for them.

I was never so glad to get out of a place! Yet, Camp Kysoc taught me things I couldn't have learned anywhere else. It also awakened in me memories of childhood and growing up in a home where we children were forbidden to say unkind things about those who were different from us. When my brother Robbie once called someone "fat," he received a stern talking-to! We knew from a young age never to stare at or ask rude questions about people with disabilities. Words like "retarded," "weird," or "ugly" were not to be used.

My mother's friend Pat, who'd had polio as a child, wore a leg brace. Mom was protective of her friend, whose leg had atrophied, causing her to walk with a terrible limp. Perhaps inspired by this friendship, Mom told me, "People with disabilities are no different from us. They have to live with something very hard, and we need to be sympathetic to their struggles."

Looking back from the perspective of Camp Kysoc, I realized my parents had sown the seeds of compassion in me very early in life. Because of it, I had always gravitated toward the "different" kids to befriend them and show them kindness. I stuck up for them when they were teased. One friend named Diane had a learning disability of some kind. She had poor vision and wore thick glasses. One day in gym class, we were told to buy gym suits and have our mothers embroider our names on them. With sadness, Diane confided in me that her mother couldn't sew. I took her uniform home with me, and Grandma Ada embroidered Diane's name on it.

Camp Kysoc was and is a tremendous blessing to thousands, giving disabled youth a beautiful, unforgettable experience. Those who were able sat around a campfire each night, roasting marshmallows and singing songs. These kids knew no other way of life than to be completely dependent upon others for everything. They were used to being cared for. Sometimes I wondered whether they ever looked at able-bodied people and felt envy. If they did, it wasn't apparent. They all seemed to smile most of the time. They were so happy to be at the camp! They radiated joy and formed friendships with other children whom they saw summer after summer.

By the time I left Camp Kysoc, I had a completely new perspective. For the first time in my life, the fact that I could walk, run, and feed myself struck me as the most amazing gift. I entered PT school with a new perspective, feeling ready to meet the challenges heading my way.

I was still the sporty, socially active young woman I'd always been. All through high school and junior college, I'd spent my hard-earned money on Villager and Ladybug clothes, penny loafers and Bass Weejuns. I arrived in Lexington to begin school with a suitcase full of fashionable wool skirts and sweaters, my hair cut in a chin-length bob.

However, I quickly found that PT school was nothing like an extension of high school or community college. The program was challenging, but thanks to the good study habits I'd developed over the past few years, I quickly figured out how to buckle down and apply myself. We PT students took our first-year classes with the first-year medical students. This

18

was serious business! I relished learning about anatomy, histology, and kinesiology alongside those future doctors who shared my passion to make a difference in the world.

In our PT class, a student named Joe had mild cerebral palsy that affected his hands. He struggled greatly to take notes during lectures. It took very little effort for me to create a copy of my notes for him by using carbon paper. That gave him good notes to study back in the dorm in the evenings, and it made me feel good to continue acting on my childhood values of helping those less fortunate than me.

As my studies intensified, I nevertheless found time to enjoy myself. I dated a medical student named Mark and found it thrilling to ride on the back of his motorcycle. Lexington sat in the middle of thoroughbred country. Mark and I zipped along the country roads through rolling hills and past perfectly manicured fields of bluegrass. Mile after mile of white wooden fences marked the boundaries around sprawling horse farms, the most notable of which was named Calumet. We stopped long enough to tour Calumet Farm. Its grandeur was eye-popping to this small-town girl who had never seen anything quite like it in her young life. The horses were off-limits, but we toured the grounds, marveling at the luxurious stables that were heated in winter and air-conditioned in summer. Injured horses even had a swimming pool for therapy! Later, when during my last semester of PT school I went to the Kentucky Derby, I remembered the pampering to which those racehorses were accustomed.

Such jaunts offered a much-needed escape from the bowels of the medical library, in which I must have spent literally hundreds of hours. I was twenty years old, and serious about my studies while simultaneously eager for a good time. The lush Kentucky springtime reminded me of Belleville, where creeks, woods, and corn and soybean fields had surrounded me. But I couldn't stay a carefree young student forever. Eventually I began dating a fellow PT student named Jack Wing, and the relationship turned into commitment. Jack was older than me, and a serious student. Following his example, I buckled down and focused on preparing myself for the career that awaited me.

Chapter Two

From Racehorses to Rehab: The Ward of Tears

During our last year in the physical therapy program, we students had to do a clerkship in the Lexington area to acquire more hands-on skills in working with patients. So, along with my rigorous studies, I spent one month doing unpaid work in a local medical facility. Cardinal Hill Rehabilitation Hospital in Lexington was a facility for people with spinal cord injuries, and I quickly gave it a nickname: The Ward of Tears.

When I opened the doors and walked into Cardinal Hill for the very first time, an overwhelming sadness descended on me. I saw bed after bed lined up in a large communal space, each one containing a young person who would never again be able to walk. Scattered among them, hidden away in their own rooms, were a scant handful of young women.

Why so many more men than women? These were the victims of car crashes, all-terrain vehicle accidents, diving accidents, and falls from great heights while doing daredevilish stunts. Data gathered on spinal cord injuries tells us that young men participate in risky activities far more often than young women. When I looked around and saw that almost all the patients fell into my age group, my heart sank.

This wasn't going to be good. I walked through the ward, a healthy, mobile twenty-one-year-old, seeing sad faces all around me—the faces of young people cut down in their prime. Some were quadriplegic and some were paraplegic. One wheelchair-bound girl with short blonde hair and swollen ankles wore white compression hose to help her circulation. She'd been in a car accident. *That could have been me*, I thought with a shudder, thinking about all the times I'd ridden in cars without wearing a seatbelt. In 1972, seatbelts were only just beginning to be required.

Not only were these people never going to walk again, but my studies had taught me that they were likely not to live to a ripe old age. Paralysis brings with it a host of other problems such as recurrent urinary tract infections, respiratory problems, and skin ulcers.

What can I possibly do for these people? I thought as I gave them fake smiles, trying to hide the uncertainty in my eyes. *Just hold steady, Martha,* I told myself. *You can do anything for one month.* The aides that cared for the patients, many of them young like me, didn't seem to share my ambivalence. They remained upbeat, laughing, smiling, and joking as they tossed balls back and forth with paraplegics, trying to build their upper body strength.

"Hey, dude, you're looking strong today!" they'd say. "Try it again!"

I had to work extra hard to feign a cheerful attitude. These patients' limbs were wasting away, and I detected a haunted expression in some of their eyes. I quickly learned that some accident victims adjust better than others to life-changing injuries.

Far too often, I had no idea what to say to them. One incredibly handsome young man named Dave had been swimming in a lake not far from Lexington when he dove off a cliff and slammed his head into a rock hidden in the murky water below. As I read his chart, I remembered my foolhardy trips to the strip-mine lakes near Belleville. My friends and I had jumped and splashed in uncharted water, exposing ourselves to all kinds of danger. It could have been me!

Dave, with his black hair and gorgeous blue eyes, was a stark reminder of human fragility. His head injury had almost turned him into a quadriplegic, but luckily for him, he had regained limited function in his upper body. He didn't have full strength, but he could shrug his shoulders, bend his elbows, and use his hands. He could breathe on his own, and that was a blessing. That minimal function made it possible for him to learn to transfer himself from one place to another.

The aides brought the patients to me in the PT gym. Using a transfer belt around Dave's waist, I managed to get him onto a mat-covered low table with the help of one of the muscular aides. I took Dave's extremities through range of motion and helped him work with hand weights. He could use his biceps, but not his triceps. I stretched out his legs, hips, knees, and back so they would grow and stay flexible enough to allow him to one day transfer in and out of a car.

These people had a tendency to get infected decubitus ulcers, more commonly known as bedsores, on their bottoms because they spent too much time sitting. The best cushions and sheepskins in the world barely served to keep the pressure off their bony hips. Because of muscle inactivity, most of them had grown extremely thin, with not nearly enough padding to protect their bones from pressure.

Now and then, I caught a glimpse of a patient crying. That's why I began to call it the "Ward of Tears." Dave remained upbeat in my presence if a bit wistful. One day, while I was bending his leg up and down at the knee, he said, "What you're doing reminds me of fetching water at the pump on my grandpa's farm in eastern Kentucky." Inwardly, my heart ached at the thought that he would never again be able to do so.

My injured patients ran the gamut between unrealistic expectations and despair. Some of those at Cardinal Hill labored under the delusion that they would one day get better. "I'm tough; I'll beat this," they said. "I'm going to work hard. You'll see!" But there is no returning from such catastrophic injury. A few young men in their thirties were married and had a child or two at home. Their sexual function was gone or severely restricted, and they were inconsolable. They would not father any more children, nor would they provide for their households in the way they had envisioned.

Other patients felt hounded by regret. *How stupid of me to drive so fast around that curve! Why did I jump into that water from so high up? What a dumb-ass thing to do!*

No matter how often I returned to Cardinal Hill, I could not shake the dark cloud of depression that seemed to hover over me there. Every time I left the place, I breathed a silent prayer of thanks that I could walk. Never again would I take my physical abilities for granted. Every day, I knew I would walk out of the facility, jump in my car, and drive away— something the patients there could only dream of doing. Their lives would never be the same.

I wondered how many tears fell at night when the patients lay alone with their thoughts in the dark, when therapy sessions were done for the week, and visitors went home. There was little comfort to be found in an environment of sterile white walls and ugly linoleum floors.

The atmosphere wasn't pretty, and neither was the daily care of a paralyzed person. No matter how modest a patient was, they had to accept the reality of exposure of their bodies to caregivers. They couldn't bathe themselves. Surely it felt degrading and humiliating to be hosed off by someone else after using the toilet! I pitied their plight yet took my cues from the aides whose unrelenting cheer encouraged the patients.

"Dave, today's your day, man. You're going to lift ten pounds. I just know it!"

Those PT exercise aides showed me how important it was to stay upbeat. I realized I wasn't going to do Dave or the other patients any good by moping around, feeling sorry for him and being depressed about his condition. I had to focus on his future. The goal of physical therapy is to help an individual get into the best shape they can within the parameters of their physical disability. When I focused on that, I found myself feeling lighter.

While in Cardinal Hill, the patients didn't have to deal with life on life's terms. They were in an artificial setting, surrounded by cheerful aides and other people with injuries like theirs. They were cared for all day long, with meals provided, their garments washed, and their bedsheets changed.

Soon they would go home to face the reality of living with their catastrophic injuries. At that point, we physical therapists heard things like, "I can't get my damn wheelchair through the door!" and "My dad is going to have to rebuild the whole bathroom." Perhaps one of the hardest things for those in wheelchairs to adjust to is having to look up to talk to people. It's as if they suddenly become five years old again, tugging on an adult's sleeve to get their attention. The paralyzed person used to stand shoulder to shoulder with others, looking them in the eye, but now everyone else in the room is looking down at them from above. Some people will avoid them altogether, not knowing what to say.

A paralyzed person can often feel invisible.

Figuring out how to proceed after release from the rehabilitation facility is a complex and frustrating process for both the patient and their family. It takes a caring, dedicated family to see to it that their son, daughter, brother, father, or spouse gets to their therapy sessions and doctor's appointments. Those with money can afford to hire in-home help, and that can ease the tension in a home. Others have no choice but to provide the injured person with the intricate daily care themselves so necessary to their survival and well-being.

Cardinal Hill was an eye-opening place for a young woman with a grandiose notion of her own efficacy. *Wow, I'm going to make the lame walk. I'm going to be so good at this!* Although I went in with thoughts like that, I came out with a healthy respect for the limits of my profession. I gained tremendous respect for the PT aides who braved the Ward of Tears every single day and did physically and mentally demanding work while simultaneously cheering up the patients. They provided excellent care! By watching them, I learned how to handle severely injured, paralyzed people. Without those aides, I certainly wouldn't have known what to do.

My clerkship at Cardinal Hill had a profound impact on me. It touched my heart deeply and also helped me know which direction to take regarding my future. After one month, I realized rehabilitation center work was a calling—one I did not have. I felt nothing but the deepest respect for those who felt called to places like the Ward of Tears, but if I was going to make a career of physical therapy, I would have to work with patients in whom I could see improvement.

Chapter Three

Formidable Flo

Before we PT graduates could be turned loose upon the world, we had to complete a series of three summer internships, during which we worked without pay. Presented with a list, we chose our destinations; one had to be in Kentucky and two out of state. Each internship lasted one month. The point of these internships was to give us experience working in other cities and different medical environments. My boyfriend Jack and I decided to do ours together, so in June of 1972, we loaded our suitcases into his car and took off for Ohio.

At Good Samaritan Hospital in Cincinnati, we learned to work in acute care, dealing with freshly injured patients. The vast facility frightened me. As a small-town girl, I'd never even stepped into such a large hospital, and now I was expected to find my way around Good Sam's endless floors and corridors. Yet the building didn't scare me nearly as much as the physical therapy department head, whose name was Florence. When she was out of earshot, we called her "Formidable Flo."

Sixty years old and tough as nails, Flo had been practicing PT for forty years, many of them spent in the Army. She was anything but warm and fuzzy. She carried herself with a military bearing and barked out orders like a drill sergeant in her strong Brooklyn accent. I felt as though I should salute her when she walked into a room. She ran Good Sam's PT department with military precision, and she intimidated me because I was more of a low-key, "go with the flow" type of girl, and I feared I could never live up to her exacting standards. Flo ran a tight ship. All our PT notes had to be in perfect order, and I feared making a mistake or looking like I didn't know what I was doing . . . which I didn't!

Ruling over a staff of ten licensed physical therapists plus an army of aides, Flo appeared to be in her element in the 1000-bed hospital. She was short and stocky of build, with close-cropped, graying hair. In those days, female therapists had to wear pantyhose, nursing oxfords, and white dresses with a triangle-shaped PT patch on them, but I got the impression Flo might have felt more comfortable in Army fatigues. I would have too, for that matter, because dresses were impractical for the type of work we did. The dress revealed

Flo's muscular calves and arms to us, and we stood in awe of the physical strength she had developed over the decades of working with injured patients.

Flo terrified us. It was her job to do so; she wasn't there to be our friend, and she came across as rock-hard because she had no time to be otherwise and still got the job done. She depended on a constant stream of interns to cover all the patients in that massive hospital. The other interns and I were so afraid of getting called into her office and being chewed out for doing the wrong thing, like accidentally hurting a patient or failing to write down complete notes. But the only time Flo ever spoke to me personally was when she saw me working out in the PT gym during a break. She came close and read my name tag.

"Why are you doing that, Martha?"

Timidly I told her I wanted to stay in shape to set an example for my patients. She accepted my answer and moved on.

Under Flo's tutelage, I put into practice what I had learned about using a tilt table. We strapped our patients onto the contraption like Dr. Frankenstein with his monster, then tilted them up with a hand crank for various reasons. My biggest fear was of messing up and not having those straps tight enough. I could just imagine a patient plummeting to the floor! I also feared taking them up too fast and making them puke.

We had to make rounds in the cavernous hospital, which to me felt like a corn maze from which I might never emerge. With no computers back then, we had to approach the nurses' station on each floor and ask to see the patients on our list. "Yeah, she's over there in room 302," they would answer, pointing to a row of hanging aluminum charts. I had to study a twenty-page chart to understand the patient's condition, then enter a complete stranger's room and figure out how to do the best I could without making their injury worse. I found it nerve-wracking!

Having Jack nearby during that month in Cincinnati was comforting, although we didn't see each other much except at work. Men and women were housed separately. He drove me to the hospital each morning, and I made use of that brief time together to bolster my confidence. Being ten years older than me, Jack served as a sounding board for this young, inexperienced kid. Physical therapy was a change of careers for him; he'd already been out in the working world, and he had a sense of calm and confidence that I could only envy. When I wasn't quite sure what to do for a patient, I consulted with him, and he gave me good advice. In fact, Jack probably got rave reviews from Flo at the end of the internship when we were all evaluated. I wasn't so sure I would. I quaked with fear whenever we gathered around Flo at our patient conferences.

"Martha, what did you do with the patient Mary Smith? What is her program?"

I lived in fear of saying the wrong thing in front of Flo and everyone else. Flo probably sensed my timidity and wrote me up as lacking confidence in patient care. If she did, I couldn't blame her; I was very young and just starting to get my feet wet in the practice of my profession. My internship in Cincinnati taught me valuable lessons and helped to launch me into the big, scary world.

By the time I left Good Samaritan, I felt only slightly more at ease in Formidable Flo's presence. None of us interns wanted to be in her sphere if we could help it. We avoided her. But that no-nonsense woman prepared me well for the future. I left Cincinnati feeling no fonder of her than when I'd arrived, yet I was grateful for the toughening-up I'd received under her supervision. I would need it for my next internship in a locked ward in Dayton, Ohio.

Chapter Four

The Locked Ward

June came to an end and once again, Jack and I packed up his car and drove to Dayton for our July internship. This time, we were assigned to a Veterans Administration hospital that just happened to have plenty of psychiatric patients who needed physical therapy. Today, we would call their condition "post-traumatic stress disorder," or PTSD. At the VA in Dayton, we saw several men struggling with PTSD, as well as nonpsychiatric outpatients who came in because of injuries or surgeries.

Some of our patients were in a locked ward because they posed a danger either to themselves or others. A few were young; most were much older, having served in the Korean War or World War II. I dreaded entering that ward, with its sign that read, *Lock the door when you leave. Key required for entrance.* In contrast, I looked forward to seeing my outpatients, with their non-threatening knee and shoulder injuries or surgeries. I knew they would improve as I worked with them, and I enjoyed talking with them about their lives outside the hospital.

Still, like a dark and haunted house, the locked ward awaited me. It felt ominous to have to ask the charge nurse to unlock the door to let me inside. The first time I watched a nurse turn the key in the lock, I wondered what would happen to me when I entered. I soon realized I had little reason to worry. The men were so heavily sedated that I wasn't expected to do anything but take them for walks.

"Hello, Mr. Jones, I'm Martha," I would say. "I'm your therapist today. We're going to go for a stroll together." Some of them shuffled along beside me, barely cognizant of their surroundings, merely going through the motions. Others were zombie-like from medication. These men didn't necessarily have physical issues. They were mental patients who needed a brief change of scenery, a bit of physical exercise, and a friendly face to smile at them. I performed my duties, then breathed a sigh of relief when I summoned the nurse to let me out.

At the VA hospital, I had a rude awakening in having to work with patients who had severe respiratory problems. These old soldiers belonged to a generation of heavy smokers. A few of the oldest ones may have breathed in mustard gas in France during World War I. They received breathing treatments. Some had tracheostomies, and many coughed up phlegm. If I had ever been tempted to smoke, working in that respiratory ward would surely have cured me of it.

The whole thing grossed me out. I did range of motion with the men's limbs as they lay in their beds and I had them roll over onto their stomachs so I could do percussion on their backs to loosen up the stubborn phlegm. In all my young life, I'd never had to deal with other people's bodily fluids; in fact, the lack of desire to do so had made me specifically *not* want to go into nursing. But it was time for me to grow up. I had to find it within myself to do what was necessary to help these patients.

"It's gross," I told myself matter-of-factly, "but this person needs it, so I have to do it. Suck it up and do your job, Martha!"

Neal, the therapist in charge of the PT department at the VA hospital, seemed to have reached an attitude bordering on indifference after having been there too long. He was over it! The job undoubtedly offered great benefits, so he'd hung around, but his mind was clearly elsewhere as he sat hunched over his desk, reading the newspaper. Neal was in his late forties. He looked professional in his white coat but remained aloof and detached from the patients, preferring to let his aides and interns deal with them. "OK, Tim," he'd call out to an exercise aide, keeping his eyes on the newspaper. "Do ten more repetitions with Mr. Brown, then do some range of motion and call it a day."

"All right, now put Mr. Green on the machine," he'd call out as he turned to the sports section. "Have him do thirty reps of knee extension and flexion."

I can't say the overly relaxed atmosphere in the department bothered me. After working for Formidable Flo, it felt pretty good to have a disengaged department head. Neal's whole demeanor said, "Whatever." He was happy to have me and Jack there to help pick up the workload, and nothing seemed to strike him as urgent. Neal's crewcut hinted at a possible military background, but little of a soldierly bearing remained about him.

The same could be said of the men in the locked ward. If they had been tall, proud soldiers once, they were now anything but. They looked defeated and disheveled. These men walked with sagging shoulders and a shuffling gate. Their eyes were dull, their expressions flat. None appeared violent or agitated. Instead, they seemed resigned. After a while, I wondered why these shadows of their former selves needed to be locked up. Might they wander away, or become violent? If so, I saw no evidence of it. Stooped, forced to wear undignified hospital gowns, they passively allowed me to lead them up and down the hospital's echoing corridors.

I read their charts and saw that most of the men were receiving shock therapy for depression and anxiety. They were extraordinarily thin, having lost muscle mass from lying around all day. I never saw any family members visiting, although I did catch glimpses of loved ones' photographs near their beds—here a lovely wife, there a couple of kids smiling out of school portraits. Did the men ever actually see these dear ones anymore? My heart broke for them. The locked ward felt like a prison with little chance of escape, and I felt claustrophobic inside it.

This internship involved almost no true physical therapy. All I did was take the men for walks, and God knows, if I didn't show up each day, they probably wouldn't have walked at all, because the facility was short-staffed. As we shuffled along, I made small talk and tried my best to fill in the silence. Some of them responded with faint smiles, a word or two, and a barely discernible nod of the head.

Each man was someone's child, husband, father, brother. Who loved them? Who missed them?

As the days wore on, a feeling of hopelessness increasingly crept over me. *Will Mr. Green ever get out of here?* I wondered. *What possible good can I do for him?* I wondered what would happen to them all when July drew to a close and I left the ward for the last time. Would another PT intern come to take my place? I hoped so. Otherwise, they would see only a distracted doctor making hasty rounds, and the nurses in white hats who tipped paper cups filled with pills into patients' mouths.

The men dutifully swallowed their medication and lifted their eyes to droning television sets suspended from the walls. They dwelt two to a room, but they did not converse with one another. They must have had stories to tell, yet those remained locked deep inside. I couldn't bear it. I told myself that these were human beings worthy of respect. They'd been heroes once. Now they were people I could work with and learn from, and perhaps my smile was a spark that added a bit of interest to the tedium of their days.

When I walked out of there on the final day of my internship, I convinced myself that the men in the locked ward would all get better one day, and then they would go home. It likely wasn't true, but some lies are necessary to keep a naïve and idealistic young woman moving in the right direction.

Chapter Five

Chattanooga

Midwestern humidity had always felt unbearable to me, but when Jack and I arrived in Chattanooga, Tennessee, for our third and final summer internship, I quickly realized those Southern Illinois summers had been child's play. From the time I entered Chattanooga to the time I left it, a wall of thick, hot, wet air enveloped me in an unwanted hug.

The city had horrible air pollution. I felt that if someone handed me a knife, I could cut that humid, polluted atmosphere into solid pieces. Together, the pollution and the humidity conspired to block out the sun, so we walked around in a shadowy pall even at midday.

When Jack dropped me off at my new temporary residence, I climbed out of the car and gazed up in wonder. A stately antebellum home had been turned into an old-fashioned girls' boarding house. While Jack and the other male interns would stay in another locale, I, as the only female, would take up residence in a little room in this once-splendid mansion. It felt to me like something out of *Gone with the Wind*!

Despite retaining its columns and expansive front porch, little of the house's former glory remained. The white exterior paint was peeling, as were the warped, black-painted shutters. The place had undoubtedly been someone's home before becoming a hotel and then a boarding house, but over the years, utility won out over plush elegance. Inside, the patterned wallpaper of burgundy velvet had seen better days. It clashed with dusty, green velvet curtains from a long-ago era. The pounding of many feet had worn grooves in the wooden stairs and hallway floors. Unsightly fire extinguishers now dotted the dimly lit hallways where gas lights and oil portraits used to hang. I showed my ID at the front desk and went upstairs to unpack my things in a tiny bedroom. It contained a small chest of drawers and a twin bed with a worn mattress on creaky springs.

Inside, the humid air felt overpowering. To fight it, I had only an electric fan so ancient it didn't even have a cage around the blades. Whenever I turned it on, I jumped back and stayed far away, fearful of having my fingers cut off. At night, out of sheer necessity, I set the fan on a chair about one foot from my bed. Then I took a shower and lay down wet, hoping against hope that I didn't flail in my sleep and thrust my hands anywhere near the whirring blades. With time, I figured out how to sneak downstairs into the forbidden kitchen and fetch ice cubes, which I put inside a rolled towel and laid under my neck.

I always felt uneasy walking down the dark corridors in the middle of the night to go to the toilet. In the mornings, I did my best to time my trip to the bathroom and shower just right. Forgoing a shower was not an option in such a climate. So, clutching my towel and soap, I would watch for someone to leave, then run down the hall to get my turn in before going down to breakfast. These breakfasts consisted of instant coffee, boxes of cereal, and generic-tasting bread stacked neatly beside toasters. Margarine and milk were kept in a big fridge that hummed loudly. The night's cloying heat hovered over the long tables in the dining room, so I didn't even try to make conversation with anyone. As a portrait of Robert E. Lee gazed down on me, I ate my food quickly so I could escape as quickly as possible.

We all shared a landline on the first floor, so if I needed to make a phone call, I had to wait my turn. I seldom used it.

Jack and I saw each other every day when he picked me up to drive me to work, and we often ate together in the evenings at little mom and pop restaurants serving southern food. Over the special of the day—fried chicken, chicken and dumplings, or meatloaf with collard greens, hush puppies, and iced sweet tea—we exchanged notes on the day's patients. These were often somber conversations, for our patients were disabled children.

The pediatric work at the Easter Seal Society Outpatient Clinic of Chattanooga was disturbing to me. My PT studies had centered around treating adults, and with the exception of my week at Camp Kysoc, I'd seldom been exposed to toddlers and young children with chronic conditions and severe disabilities. As an idealistic young therapist who wanted to see results, I found it depressing to work, albeit patiently and kindly, with children and see very little progress.

Although these children were darling and they tugged at my heart strings, I knew I would never have the patience to work with them long-term. Not that I felt impatient with *them*. I felt impatient and frustrated that therapy seemed to do so little to change their circumstances. Most of the children would not improve much, and I found that depressing.

I quickly learned that any PT who works with disabled children has to be in it for the long haul. The kids' progress is incremental. They make strides in teeny, tiny, baby steps. Some of the patients were so young that it broke my heart. Many were confined to wheelchairs. I got down on the floor with them on foam mats to follow the head therapist's instructions and work with these little ones to strive to reach basic milestones like sitting, rolling over, and crawling—all things parents of healthy children take for granted.

As at Camp Kysoc, a majority of the children had cerebral palsy in its various forms. A few had chromosomal abnormalities such as Down's syndrome. A couple suffered from spina bifida. Some were blind in addition to the other effects of cerebral palsy. Some couldn't hear. Some had been damaged at birth or in utero. Leg braces were common in those days, and many of our patients had them. Many of them wore helmets to protect their heads from falls or seizures.

Observing the woman in charge, I felt overwhelming admiration for her kindness and patience. She had a true calling to work with these children. It occurred to me that one needed to feel called to such work in order to spend every day with complex and multi-faceted cases. Not only did the children have physical abnormalities, but they had a host of other complications, including being unable to swallow and needing a feeding tube. These were severely involved children with needs in swallowing, speech, and vision. It all felt too overwhelming to me.

Thankfully, I could debrief with Jack over dinner in the evenings. On weekends, we packed up peanut butter sandwiches and enjoyed picnics in one or the other of Chattanooga's pretty, public parks. We tried our best to ignore the oppressive humidity as we walked around or just sat on benches, soaking in the lush, verdant scenery.

Camp Kysoc and the Easter Seal Clinic bookended my PT education—Kysoc at the very beginning and Chattanooga at the end. This exposure to pediatric therapy showed me that I didn't have what it took to do it long-term. Any PT who worked with such disabled children would need to persevere at it for years. Because of my grandmother Ada's misfortune, my heart was set on working with outpatients who would get better. I felt more drawn to orthopedics or even geriatrics, and knew I was better suited to it than to pediatrics. At least if an elderly patient was struggling with a degenerative condition, I could console myself that they had had a long life.

I knew I would do better in an environment where I could assess an adult patient, then formulate a plan based on my diagnosis. Hip surgery was no mystery to me. I knew exactly how to treat someone who'd had strained their shoulder. Adult patients could talk to me, let me know how they were feeling, whereas the children at the clinic often couldn't communicate with us. I left Chattanooga with the utmost admiration for any physical therapist who felt called to work with these precious but challenging kids.

Of course, I wasn't so naïve as to imagine that all the patients in my future would improve. I just hoped that most of them would! As I packed up to leave Chattanooga behind, I wondered what challenges awaited me. Just ahead lay the receipt of my diploma and my first real job as a physical therapist.

PART II

Back to Belleville

We rise by lifting others.

—Robert Ingersol

Chapter Six

Ellen's Lymphedema

My patient tried to hide her grotesquely swollen arm beneath a crocheted sweater draped over her shoulders. The sheer bulk of it horrified her. Expanded to three times its normal size, Ellen's left arm had fallen victim to a common villain during the 1970s—a mastectomy. Back then, surgeons tended to remove all the armpit's lymph glands right along with the breast. Since the lymph system drains excess fluid from the body, breast cancer patients were often left with lymphedema, a condition in which fluid accumulates in the hand and arm. Ellen suffered terribly from this painful and embarrassing condition.

In her late sixties, Ellen was a slender, stylish woman who paid meticulous attention to her hair and make-up. She should have been active in her church and neighborhood social circles as she recovered from her surgery. Doctors had given her an excellent prognosis, and she had every reason to continue her career as a seamstress who operated her own alteration business, because her quality workmanship was well-known around Belleville. Instead, she found herself staying home, hiding from the world.

Ellen brushed a lock of curly, white hair from her eyes as she smiled and told me all about her daughters and how she had sewn all their clothes as they were growing up. As she spoke, memories of happier times put a smile on her face . . . until she remembered her condition and her eyes dropped to her swollen arm. "I just don't even want to appear in public anymore," she sighed. "And I don't know how much longer I'll be able to sew. I'm a widow, and that's why I turned my hobby into a business—to supplement my social security. But my arm is so swollen that sewing has become painful!"

At age twenty-two, with a great job and my whole life ahead of me, I could hardly imagine what it might feel like to be an elderly widow trying to scrape by financially. I certainly didn't know then that my husband would die of cancer, leaving me a widow at a young age myself. But I felt keenly the sorrow in Ellen's heart and detected fear in her voice. What would life look like if she couldn't earn the extra money necessary to take care of herself? And her arm did look alarmingly grotesque!

I understood the science behind Ellen's condition—the swelling from her lymphedema was putting pressure on the nerves and causing terrible pain. Should she be so unlucky as to brush her arm against something sharp and scratch it, it could become severely infected. The surgery that had maimed her had been necessary to remove cancer, and the loss of her lymph glands could never be reversed. Thankfully, however, I was armed with the knowledge of something that could bring Ellen relief.

Over the past few years, Don had noticed we were getting more and more lymphedema-after-mastectomy patients in the physical therapy department at Belleville Memorial Hospital. Because of this, he'd called me aside one day and said, "Martha, I've been reading about the Jobst Institute in Toledo, Ohio. They're making some fabulous, new compression sleeves for woman with lymphedema of the arm. I want you to go there and take a course on their products. Come back and lead the way in how to use those products for our patients."

I felt honored to be asked to do this. The hospital paid my way to Toledo, and as I traveled, I had a strong sense of purpose. Being entrusted with this task validated me as a physical therapist. As a young, recent graduate from PT school who was often uncertain about my abilities, I needed this confidence boost!

As I toured the Jobst Institute facility, I learned that Conrad Jobst, a mechanical engineer and inventor born in Germany, had suffered from severe, chronic venous insufficiency of both legs, resulting in terrible varicose veins and stasis ulcers. Jobst put his engineering skills to work as he set about trying to find a solution. If he could experiment on himself, he reasoned, he just might be able to improve not only his own circumstances but also improve the lives of other people.

While touring the beautiful indoor swimming pool at the Jobst Institute, I saw patients walking up and down its lanes through the water. Conrad Jobst had discovered that one of the few things that gave him relief was being in a pool of chest-high water. The water exerted pressure on his body, alleviating his symptoms. Because of this hydro-pressure, people can do things in water they can't do on land. It occurred to Jobst that if he could replicate that pressure outside of the water, he and others like him might experience lasting improvement. Jobst was desperate for a cure. Walking had become excruciatingly painful; his ankles and legs were terribly swollen.

Out of this discovery, Jobst invented the compression stocking to prevent blood clots, using a pressure gradient system. He knew that if he could create an external pressure on the legs or arms, he could duplicate what happens in water. We use these compression stockings and sleeves to this day, and they work! They relieve pain. They accomplish on the exterior of the body what the internal veins are unable to do. He founded JOBST in Toledo in 1950, and after his death, his wife Caroline grew the business. By the time I visited Toledo, sales extended to virtually every continent.

In Toledo I learned that all the Jobst support sleeves and stockings are created uniquely for each patient. We were taught how to make specific measurements of a person's limb, then send the measurements to the Jobst Institute, where they would create a garment accordingly. This was revolutionary! I brought this information back to Belleville with me, feeling as though I were transporting a secret weapon.

Modern medicine had cured Ellen of cancer but left her with a terrible disability. Not only was her swollen arm weak and painful, but it was too heavy to lift and move around. Because of what I'd learned at Jobst, I knew I could help her. I put her on an exercise program, but more importantly, I measured her from the tips of her fingers to her shoulder.

When the flesh-colored sleeve arrived from Toledo, we wrestled it onto Ellen's arm. Immediately it began to act as a pump, doing what her lymph system could no longer do for her. As it pushed the fluids out, I also massaged her arm. I had her lie back on the table, lifted her arm up, and, resting her hand on my shoulder, I pushed that fluid toward her heart. Ellen always felt better when she left, because her shoulder and elbow were becoming stiff from all that fluid.

The first time she wore the sleeve, Ellen said, "Oh, my gosh! My arm feels so good!"

I instructed Ellen to elevate her arm three to four times a day to let gravity assist in bringing the fluids toward her heart. Over time, I measured her for three different sleeves as the size of her arm changed because of reduced swelling. Ellen would have to wear the sleeve for the rest of her life, but that seemed a minor inconvenience compared to the misery she had suffered before. In the summer, the sleeve would be hot and uncomfortable. Ellen didn't mind. Without the sleeve, her swelling was sure to come back and in no way did she want that to happen. Ellen's arm never went back to its previous size, but it did get to a place where it looked pretty close to normal. She found she could sew and do everything she had done before her mastectomy.

Over the years, I fitted many people with Jobst sleeves and stockings. I found there was no comparison between those made-to-order sleeves and generic ones from drug stores. And as time passed, I noticed a decline in radical mastectomies, especially those that included removal of all the lymph nodes. Today, more lumpectomies are performed, and only the lymph nodes containing cancer cells are removed.

Jobst has now expanded into other products, making stockings for amputees' stumps, gloves for people with severe hand injuries, and pneumatic boots and sleeves. Conrad Jobst used his own suffering to benefit thousands if not millions of people all over the world. I'm honored to have been one of the many people who brought, and still bring, his invention to

those he intended to help.

Chapter Seven

The Frozen Shoulder That Wouldn't Thaw

Freshly out of physical therapy school and hired by Don, the very man who had tried to discourage me from entering the field in the first place, I showed up for my new job at Memorial Hospital in Belleville, Illinois, ready to practice my profession. Although I may have projected confidence, inside I was nervous. Patients were going to be put into my, what seemed to me, less than capable hands. Would I remember all that I had learned? Would I go too far and hurt someone? Would I not go far enough and leave them wishing they hadn't wasted their time coming to physical therapy?

Don took my youth and inexperience into consideration. He gave me easier patients at first, and Barbara Steinberg seemed to fit that description. Barbara, the wife of a judge, lived in a beautiful home in Country Club Heights with a large garden—her pride and joy. Day after day, she dug holes for new trees, pruned rose bushes, pulled weeds, harvested vegetables. She raked and mowed, preferring to do the work herself though she could easily have afforded to hire a gardener. The repetitive motions took their toll on her right shoulder, and she presented to me in severe pain, having waited far too long to see her doctor about the problem. Instead, she'd relied upon aspirin until it was no longer effective.

"My shoulder feels frozen," she told me. "I can't even reach up into my kitchen cupboard to get baking ingredients anymore."

Barbara was in her late fifties, attractive and well put together in an understated sort of way. With her sleek haircut and classic, expensive clothing, she oozed the kind of elegance and confidence of the wealthy and prominent. I'd felt immediately nervous upon learning her husband's profession, thinking, *I'd better be careful! If I do something wrong, I might get in serious trouble!* Barbara was the first wealthy patient I ever saw, and ridiculously, I feared she might somehow break if I touched her the wrong way.

Eager to make a good impression, I set about gingerly doing range of motion to measure just how far the affected shoulder would allow Barbara's arm to rotate. Then I applied hot packs and massaged the joint. I stretched her arm gently, then more aggressively. I showed her how to "climb the wall" by gradually reaching higher and higher and admonished her to do all her exercises faithfully at home.

As a young therapist in my early twenties, I couldn't help but be prone to self-doubt. Barbara had placed herself in my hands and in doing so, showed a tremendous amount of trust. Here she was, a fifty-year-old woman, and I looked nineteen at the most! Even as she had made a conscious choice to trust me, I had to learn to trust myself.

Barbara kept coming back to see me, but all my efforts helped her very little. The shoulder, like the hip, wrist, and ankle, is a complicated joint because it has so many motions. One can make circles with it. It's the rotator cuff that allows this circular movement, and the connective tissue on Barbara's was so tight she could barely move her arm. One month later, she showed little progress, though I had tried my hardest. "I don't know if I'll ever be able to garden again," she said. I began to feel as though I'd failed her.

That's when Barbara's orthopedist, Dr. Hurd, decided to do something radical. He admitted Barbara to the hospital, put her under anesthesia, and manipulated her arm. Had she been awake, she would have screamed and fainted from the pain. Don watched the procedure and later told me that as Dr. Hurd pulled and twisted her arm, he could hear all the adhesions in her shoulder popping loose. "Martha, there is no way you, or anyone else, could have accomplished that by doing regular physical therapy," he assured me.

Barbara came out of the procedure swollen and in tremendous pain, but relieved. The procedure worked! Now it was up to me to strengthen Barbara's shoulder and keep it from freezing up again. While recovering in the hospital, she kept ice packs on the shoulder and came down to the PT department four times a day, where I worked with her to steadily increase her range of motion.

After she left the hospital, Barbara continued to see me as an outpatient until all her shoulder's function was eventually restored. I used a form of dry heat called diathermy, as well as therapeutic ultrasound. And naturally, I massaged her shoulder. Nothing can beat therapeutic touch to help a patient on their way to healing.

In those days with no computers, I had to sit down at an old-fashioned typewriter in an office I shared with the other PTs and type out an exercise program for my patients. With no secretary to do it for me, I had to use my lunch break or stay after work to get this important part of my job accomplished. I put Barbara on a very specific program and as with all my other patients, I regularly asked her to show me what she was doing at home so I could know she was following through correctly. If a patient improved, I knew they were doing their exercises. I considered myself a coach. In fact, to me, PT not only stands for physical therapy, but for "personal trainer."

What happened with Barbara would almost surely never happen today. Insurance companies were different back then; patients used to be admitted to the hospital for frozen shoulders or back pain, and many other orthopedic problems. Insurance paid for it all! A procedure such as Barbara's under anesthesia would be unheard of now because it would be far too expensive, considering the surgeon's bill, the anesthesiologist's bill, and hospital costs. That's unfortunate, because it was highly effective.

We may have figured out many new and effective ways of doing things, but have we really made progress? Back in the 1970s, insurance would pay for a patient to see a physical therapist for as long as six months if that's what it took to heal.

It was a different time indeed.

Chapter Eight

More Than Just a Total Knee

Well, I'll be darned, I thought when I glanced at my new patient's paperwork. *There aren't too many people around here named Kurrus, so she must be from the Kurrus family. And wow, I've never seen anyone with a total knee before. A brand-new joint . . . oh, this will be a snap!*

The Kurruses had buried my family members for four generations. Their funeral parlor in Belleville had been around since the early 1900s, just like Hill Thomas Lime and Cement, our family business. As business owners, our forefathers had surely had occasion to socialize or at least meet each other. Of course, that didn't mean my patient, Mabel Kurrus, would have a clue who I was. I planned to go about my work as usual and prepared to introduce myself to her.

For some reason, I was feeling confident that day. I now had a few months of practice under my belt and if I said so myself, I had a special touch with elderly patients. I just knew Mabel would love me. *All* the older patients did!

Charles Kurrus, the mortician, stood beside his wife's wheelchair. He and Mabel, a petite, sixty-year-old woman with short, wavy gray hair and sparkling diamond studs in her earlobes, looked at me somewhat skeptically. The couple continued to watch me closely, saying very little. After we introduced ourselves, I explained to Mabel what I was going to do to her leg. As I spoke, I began to unwrap the ACE bandage around her knee.

"Do you think my surgeon wants you to unwrap this knee?" she suddenly asked, looking me squarely in the eye.

I stared at her, my mouth hanging open.

Mabel went on to say, "I went all the way to Chicago to get this knee replacement, and I don't want to go back there and have it done again. So, maybe you should call my surgeon and find out exactly what you should be doing."

My face went hot, then cold, then hot again. I broke out in a sweat. Oh, how I hoped nobody in the department had overheard this humiliating conversation with frail, tiny Mabel Kurrus! I stopped what I was doing, mumbled something that didn't make much sense, and quickly wheeled her into an examination room and pulled the curtain. I fetched a chair for

Charles. Knowing I had to be completely honest with this patient, I admitted I had never before worked with a total knee replacement, and that I had only just graduated from physical therapy school within the last year.

"I really want to help you," I said. "I'll call your doctor and I won't do anything he doesn't want me to do."

Total knee replacements were new and rare in the early 1970s, but because Mabel had a son who was an internist at Rush Presbyterian Hospital in Chicago, he'd been able to find the finest surgeon to perform the surgery on his mother. She'd been in constant pain, and she could no longer go up and down the stairs of the family's stately Belleville home. She'd been so desperate that she plucked up the courage to go under the knife and have surgery so new it was almost experimental.

Mabel seemed to relax when I told her I would call her surgeon. She looked up at my nametag and said, "You're Martha Thomas! I believe I know your parents and grandparents. And Charles's grandfather knew your great-grandparents. Your grandparents were friends of our family for years . . . years ago."

"Wow," I said, and heaved a sigh of relief.

She smiled. "I think you and I will do just fine together. By the way, are you going to use *that thing* on me before I leave?" Mabel laughed as she said it, pointing at the goniometer sticking out of my pocket, a sharp-looking tool like a protractor with which we measured the movements of patients' joints.

"As a matter of fact, I am," I replied, feeling much more relaxed. I took her joint measurements and by the time Mabel left that day, I felt emotionally exhausted. This sharp old lady who was not about to let an inexperienced young girl mess up her knee surgery had taught me a valuable lesson. Because I had never worked with a total knee before, I should have been more prepared. I should have called her surgeon before I even saw her. Never again did I make that mistake of overblown confidence.

For the next six months, Mabel came in for physical therapy. In those days, we could see patients for that long because insurance covered it. She was so funny and very sweet to all the other patients in the gym. She did extremely well. Her surgeon said he wanted her to get a 100-degree flexion and full extension, and she did.

Mabel and I became friends over the course of her six-month therapy. More than that, she became a grandmotherly figure to me. My grandma Ada had passed away by then, and I so appreciated Mabel filling that gap in my life. By the same token, I became a surrogate granddaughter to her since her own grandchildren lived out of state. We had lunch together. She and Charles invited me over to their stately home for lunches and dinners, and we even planned outings together in St. Louis. When Mabel began to suspect I didn't know how to cook or sew, she set out to remedy that. Grandma Ada had taught me to bake some sweet treats, but I couldn't throw a meal together to save my life.

"You graduated from college, but you can't cook dinner or sew a dress?" asked Mable, astonished. "Well, Martha, it's time you learned!"

After that, I spent Sunday afternoons cutting out patterns on Mabel's living room floor, and she patiently demonstrated how to piece garments together on her sewing machine. She taught me how to preserve strawberries. One day, we put up thirty jars of strawberry jam! Mabel had so much energy and vigor that she sometimes tired me out. So did

Charles. They owned a huge property, and while Mabel and I cooked and sewed, he was often out in the yard, mowing or trimming bushes or watering plants.

Charles behaved like anything but a somber, serious mortician. He relished making jokes about his profession and even proudly went by the nickname "Digger." To formal occasions, he often wore a necktie with the image of a shovel on it. His warm and engaging personality lit up the atmosphere wherever he went, and he always made me feel so welcome in their home. Mabel and Charles were wealthy, influential people in Belleville, but they were humble and hospitable too. Their three-story, white-shuttered home, which they opened up so freely to me and to many others, sat on two acres filled with maple and oak trees in an exclusive neighborhood called Signal Hill. The house was stunningly decorated, with exquisite carpets and paintings, and a grand piano.

This close, loving couple modeled for me a happy marriage—something I had rarely seen in my own household growing up. Eventually, I introduced them to my fiancé Jack, and invited them to our wedding reception banquet. Later, after I married and moved to Phoenix, I came back to Belleville just to attend the Kurruses' fiftieth wedding anniversary celebration.

When I first saw Mabel, she was using a walker, but then she graduated to a cane. In time, she needed nothing at all, and could walk completely on her own. I advised her to take the cane out with her in public despite not needing it, because it would encourage people to keep their distance and prevent her from being bumped or jostled. People tend to give those with canes wide berth, and the last thing Mabel needed was to be knocked down.

She was a perfect patient! She did all her exercises faithfully and made excellent progress in her recovery. Of course, the fact that she lived with a wonderful man who had a great sense of humor really helped. They laughed a lot together, and laughter is healing. For me, seeing them tease each other and joke around was a beautiful thing to behold.

Mabel and I reached therapeutic goals together, but we got a lot more than that out of our partnership. We became true friends. She was exactly what I needed in my life at the time, and I became what she needed. The fact that she knew everybody in my family helped to cement that relationship. It happened organically.

"Your grandmother was a lovely person," said Mabel, "and your grandfather Bob did such wonderful things for the young men in the community. He was an excellent Sunday School teacher in our church. You should be proud to be named after your grandmother, and your brother should be proud to be named after Robert!" I'd heard stories about my grandparents from family members, of course, but it was a gift to hear it from Mabel and Charles, who had been their friends. This was as close as I would ever be able to get to my grandparents, since my grandfather Thomas died before I was born, and my grandmother Martha died when I was one year old.

In my entire forty years of practicing physical therapy, Mabel is the only patient with whom I developed a close friendship. Normally, one doesn't become friends with patients. In most situations, it's inappropriate. But with someone who knew my entire family, it felt entirely appropriate. Mabel and Charles passed away many years ago, but my happy memories of time spent with them live on. Hill

Thomas Lime and Cement closed down after 105 years, but Kurrus Funeral Home is still going strong, run by Charles and Mabel's great-grandchildren.

Chapter Nine

First, Do No Harm

Recently graduated from the challenging physical therapy program at the University of Kentucky, I found myself plagued with anxiety. How could I be sure I was doing the right thing for each of my patients? Which program would be best for this or that severely injured person? I was young and green, and each patient had a unique condition resulting from wildly varying circumstances.

Back in my hometown of Belleville, I'd just been hired by the very man who had tried to talk me out of going into the profession in the first place. Not long after I returned to live with my parents, Don, who knew our family, gave me a call. "Hey," he said. "Your mom told me you just graduated, and I want to offer you a job."

"Really? I thought you said there were too many women!"

"Well, I still think so," he admitted, "but I'm short-staffed, and I need a therapist. I'm happy to give you the job."

Don was far from being chauvinistic or a misogynist. He meant well and was merely speaking the truth from his perspective. The field of physical therapy, a nondrug medical treatment used to restore functions such as standing, walking, and movement of body parts had indeed been dominated by women for decades. In 1918, the term "reconstruction aide" was used to describe the women who were then practicing what we now call physical therapy.

The first school of physical therapy in America was established at Walter Reed Army Hospital in Washington, DC, following the onset of World War I. Mary McMillan is often considered the founding mother of the discipline. She drew upon training and education that she'd received in England when she returned to the United States to help rehabilitate survivors of the war. At Walter Reed, she led a group of eighteen women who administered exercise therapy and massage to injured troops—men who suffered from neurological injuries, multiple amputations, head injuries, PTSD, and severe pain.

After successfully rehabilitating soldiers, Mary McMillan and her fellow aides founded the American

Women's Physical Therapy Association in 1921. The association's journal, called the *PT Review*, debuted in 1921. Today, this publication is called *The Journal of the American Physical Therapy Association.*

When Franklin Delano Roosevelt contracted polio in 1921, the disease paralyzed him from the waist down. In 1926, someone introduced him to a physical therapist named Alice Plastridge, who was experienced in treating polio victims. At a rehabilitation center in Warm Springs, Georgia, Alice supervised the physical therapy treatments. Patients, including Roosevelt, received excellent care at Warm Springs, and under Alice's direction, they experienced relief and the relaxation of tightened muscles. Alice's use of exercise, massage, and especially hydrotherapy greatly benefitted polio patients as well as those with other types of paralysis.

Don couldn't deny that he owed his profession to the women who had founded it. He just thought, and rightly so, that the field could benefit from the addition of a few strong men. It took a lot of physical strength to deal with certain patients whose disabilities rendered them unable to move. As a young woman of twenty, I was tall, athletic, and slim. I may not have brought brute strength to the table, but I was well-educated and determined, and I took my responsibilities seriously. Eagerly I joined the PT staff at Memorial Hospital, feeling privileged to work with Don, his assistant department head Jay, and another young woman named Mickie.

For all my enthusiasm, I was still young, inexperienced, and wholly unprepared for the arrival of a patient named Gary.

Red-headed, freckle-faced Gary was a farmer and family man with a wife and two small children. He looked every bit the country boy in his blue flannel shirt and Levi cut-offs, the backs of his hands permanently tanned from long hours spent in the sun. That a farmer would become a patient of mine was hardly surprising, considering that Belleville was surrounded by fields of corn and soybeans stretching as far as the eye could see. The small country roads through and around those fields had been my playground as a teenager; on them, my friends and I used to drive around in the dark and stargaze, taking turns lying on top of the car's roof. It was stupid and dangerous, but I was a kid who thought I'd live forever. Undoubtedly, Gary had thought he would too. At age thirty, he certainly couldn't have anticipated the accident that would change his life so completely.

Gary, who was meant to eventually take over his father's farm along with his two brothers, was out riding a tractor one day when a rock or ditch caused the massive vehicle to flip over. It pinned Gary to the ground. Cell phones didn't exist at the time. Emergency 911 systems were not yet widespread across Illinois, and it may have taken a long time for help to arrive, or even for anyone else on the farm to realize what had happened. Gary had grown up on tractors. He knew them inside and out, but that bad turn of luck left him with a spinal cord injury at T12 that paralyzed him from the waist down.

Bright blue eyes looked up at me, framed by a fading sunburn. It had been weeks since Gary had been out in the weather. By the time he came into Memorial Hospital for rehab, planting season was over, and the crops were ripening in the sun of high summer. His earnest expression told me he was a good guy, a hard worker, someone who under normal circumstances couldn't stand to sit still and do nothing. Farming was in Gary's blood. Likely, the farm he'd grown up on and worked with his family had been passed down through several generations, and growing the food that fed a nation was a source of pride to them.

Gary had been brought straight to Memorial Hospital for treatment. He spent weeks there. Now, he came in as an outpatient, wheeled in by his wife. Two small children in overalls toddled alongside his chair. They grew excited at the sight of our gym equipment and begged to play on it, having no conception of the gravity of their father's situation.

"Hush now," said their earthy, blue-jeaned mother in a calm, patient voice. "Those are for Daddy and other people who need them. They ain't for you kids." I noticed that the little blonde-haired girl resembled her mommy while the boy was the spitting image of Gary, with bright red hair and a smattering of freckles across his nose. If Gary's wife was sad about his accident, she hid it well. Putting on a brave face, she acted as an encourager to her husband. She kissed him goodbye, took each child by the hand, and led them out of the department. It was time to get down to work.

Being assigned to work with a paralyzed person always felt like a gut punch to me. Working with people with spinal injuries can be depressing for a therapist because there is little to no chance of recovering nerve function. I knew that if I gave in to depression, the quality of my work would suffer. Getting through it was a skill I'd learned well as a child growing up in a home where alcohol played a big role, creating an environment over which I had little, if any, control. I'd had to focus on what I *could* do. Likewise, in my profession, I had to learn to ask myself, "What can I do to help this person return to the best physical life they can have under the circumstances?" Then I would focus on getting them strong and keeping them stretched out so they could return to doing what they loved in the best capacity possible.

Because of the severity of Gary's injury, he was incontinent of bowel and bladder and would never father any more children. As his son and daughter left the room, I felt happy for him that he had those two. His paralysis was irreversible, but it was his good fortune to have full use of his upper body, and I intended to strengthen his arms and teach him how to transfer himself in and out of a car, on and off a toilet, and in and out of bed so he could recover a measure of self-sufficiency. It remained to be seen whether he would be able to drive a tractor again, but hand-operated cars existed, and I felt certain Gary would eventually be able to drive the roads of St. Clair County again. To do that, he would need to be able to get himself from wheelchair to car and back to wheelchair.

The young farmer put on a brave face and tried to be cheerful, but beneath his smile, I detected a deep sadness. He'd been cut down in his prime. Most paralysis patients take some time to realize that they are never going to walk again. They pass through the stages of grief, anger, and acceptance. Gary didn't seem angry, but his depression hung like a heavy, dark cloud over him. The only hope I could offer him was to get his arms strong enough to lift the weight of his lower body so he could aim for at least independence of movement.

My position at Belleville Memorial was my first real job. I'd worked in the department before as an aide between my junior and senior year of college, and Don must have seen something in me as I prepared hot packs, scrubbed whirlpools, and prepped patients for the physical therapists. I felt vindicated that the very man who had tried to discourage my friend and me from entering the field had now hired me. He was a great boss. An ex-Marine, he sported a crew cut and a healthy physique except for a slightly bulging belly resulting from a love of ice cream. I wanted to impress Don. I wanted to prove that I could do the job every bit as well as a man so that he would have no regrets in hiring me. After all, the hospital was paying me a whopping $9,000 a year! I'd almost fainted when Don offered me that princely sum. I thought I'd hit the jackpot.

However, when Don assigned Gary to me, I immediately began to feel my old nemesis, anxiety, rise up again. My boss thought the young paraplegic would be an excellent teacher for me as I experimented and put into practice all that I had studied in books. Don didn't know that at the tender age of twenty-one, I was full of self-doubt. I hid it well. Yet I often lost sleep at night, worrying about my patients and how I was going to take care of them. I also happened to be studying late into each night for my state board exams, as well as writing letters and talking on the phone to my long-distance boyfriend Jack. As a result, I was running on little sleep. Lack of sleep fueled and increased my anxiety! It became a vicious cycle. On top of it all, my parents had separated, and I found myself living with my father, who struggled with alcoholism, in the house in which I'd grown up. The stress in our family only added to my feelings of insecurity.

Dad was a great guy. Looking back, I understand alcoholism much better, knowing it is an illness that willpower alone will not cure. My father self-medicated with alcohol to cover up feelings of inferiority and anxieties over his failed first marriage and his failing second marriage. Yet, he was kindhearted and funny, and he taught his children how to have fun. That was a quality I needed, since I tended to take my new responsibilities extremely seriously.

How thrilled I was to have that job! I needed money. I needed a car. Hoping it was only a matter of time until I gained more confidence and lost all my fear, I put one foot in front of the other, showing up to work each day determined to do my best. Fortunately, Don, Jay, and Mickie were supportive. Memorial Hospital was a perfect learning environment, with critically injured patients arriving by helicopter on a regular basis.

Unfortunately, Gary's depression was contagious. This wasn't a fun situation for him or me. Nevertheless, he had to come to terms with his condition and it was my duty to help him along in the process. I began to spend a full hour with Gary three times a week doing physically demanding work. We put Gary in long-leg braces, and I wheeled him over to the waist-high parallel bars. With much effort, he learned to pull himself up to a standing position. From there, he could practice his balance and even push down on the bars and swing his legs, which simulated walking.

Gary's upper-body strength improved greatly during my time with him. Usually wearing a white T-shirt and Bermuda shorts, he came in determined to accomplish his goals, always getting right down to work. As he grew stronger, his mood lifted. He did chest presses with a barbell and did other weight work to strengthen his upper body. Like most men, Gary looked forward to the "working out" part of his therapy. We could measure his progress, and that encouraged him. He felt like he was actually doing something to help himself, and that was a huge morale booster.

Comparison also acted as an effective morale booster. Normally we speak of comparison as a negative thing, but for the paraplegic, it can be quite therapeutic. In our PT gym, when

Gary saw stroke patients sitting in wheelchairs, barely aware of what was going on around them, he felt lucky to have all his mental faculties intact. When he caught a glimpse of quadriplegics outfitted with breathing apparatuses, he knew he was blessed to have the full use of his upper body.

The patients in our gym encouraged each other. If outpatients recovering from knee or hip surgery saw Gary lifting weights, they often said things like, "Hey, buddy, you're doing great! Keep it up!" or "You're looking good today, my man. You'll lift even more tomorrow!"

"Put Gary on the mat table," Don instructed me one day. Physical therapy was a very "physical" job in those days, and this was where being an athletic girl came in handy. With Gary helping as much as he could by using his hands and arms, I managed to get him onto the low table covered with soft, cushioned mats. After working his upper body out with weights, I started stretching out his legs to loosen up the muscles, knowing that if they got too tight, he wouldn't be able to transfer himself from chair to bed, chair to car, chair to toilet and back.

Whenever I stretched patients' limbs, I erred on the side of being too gentle out of fear of hurting them. In Gary's case, I climbed onto the mat table and put first one leg, then the other, up over my shoulder so I could push it through its range of motion and bend his knees.

Don watched me as I worked. "You've got to stretch him harder, Martha. You're doing a fine job, but you're not stretching him hard enough. Be a little more aggressive." Then he demonstrated. I watched him carefully, eager to learn and to please. The words "First, do no harm" echoed in my brain as I observed his expertise. In PT school, we had committed that mantra to memory and it guided everything I did. As I repeated the words again to myself, I thought, *Well, if Don is telling me to do it, it must be the right thing to do.*

I climbed back up and pushed and pulled harder on Gary's legs. Suddenly, I heard a loud "pop." It sounded like a crack. "What was that?" I said, knowing Gary couldn't feel anything but wondering if he'd heard the sound.

He shrugged. "I don't know, but it was really loud."

I went immediately to tell Don about the popping sound.

"Oh, it was probably just a ligament," he said. "Go ahead and stop for the day." My boss's nonchalant demeanor masked a deep suspicion. Just to be sure, he called Gary's doctor and arranged for an X-ray. Orderlies came to wheel him up to radiology and the results came back quickly. I had broken Gary's leg. I'd cracked his femur, the largest bone in the human body, right in two. I was devastated.

Don called me into his office immediately. "Martha, I don't want you to feel badly about this," he said. "Remember that Gary's bones are brittle from lack of use. This could have happened to anybody."

Standing upright and moving is what keeps our bones strong. In paralysis, they become brittle for lack of use. I understood all this, yet I felt terrible. The break caused Gary a real setback in his rehabilitation. From that moment on, I walked around with a dark cloud over my head. I had nightmares. Gary's doctor had readmitted him to the hospital because of the broken femur, and his leg was in traction. I went to visit him twice a day, every day, until he was able to get out of bed again. In tears and apologizing profusely, I told him the only thing that comforted me was that he couldn't feel any pain as a result of my terrible mistake. "I really thought I was doing the right thing," I sobbed.

Gary was nothing if not gracious. He harbored no ill will toward me. "I know this was an accident," he said. "You've done so much for me, Martha. You've taught me how to get in and out of bed, how to move myself around. I know how to get on and off a toilet now, so my wife doesn't have to help me! That's worth so much to me!" Gary and his wife continued to thank me for all the help I'd given him. He chose to look forward, eagerly anticipating driving again. He was even determined to get back up onto a tractor that was outfitted with hand controls.

For years afterward, I had nightmares about that mishap, and I considered myself lucky that Gary and his family didn't sue me. I never pushed or pulled that hard on a patient again. Never in forty years of practicing did I injure another patient in any way. Throughout the rest of my career, I became known for having an especially gentle touch. Co-workers said, "Give Martha the old patients" and "Give Martha the people who are fragile."

The incident with Gary is exactly why physical therapists are encouraged to buy expensive insurance policies. We are also encouraged to acquire disability policies at a young age, because the physical nature of the work can result in us leaving the profession due to back or shoulder injuries. In the early years of my practice, we therapists took patients to the bathroom in our PT department and cleaned them up afterward. What a strain on our bodies! Today, therapists are not expected to do such things.

There is nothing worse than sending a patient home knowing they do not have any family to support them. I didn't have to worry about that with Gary. Because a spouse plays a key role in the adjustment and progress of a paralytic, I taught Kathleen how to stretch her husband's limbs and to recognize the signs of the maladies that plague those in wheelchairs— urinary tract infections and the ulcers on the skin commonly known as bedsores. Taking care of someone confined to a wheelchair is a tough job, and sometimes the tension between spouses escalates because of caregiver burnout. That's why if people have the money to do so, I recommend hiring someone from outside to come in to care for the patient and give the spouse some relief. However, because Kathleen seemed teachable and eager to help, and because I knew they had extended family living right around them, I felt hopeful for their future.

I can only assume that Gary found a way to contribute to his family's farming enterprise. They owned a roadside fruit stand, so maybe he managed it. He might even have learned to drive the produce into St. Louis to sell to various markets. One thing is for sure—he and his wife had a strong, built-in support system. Farming families around Belleville often lived with several generations on the same property, one child living in a house here, another child living in another with his family, and so on. It was common for them all to eat at the same table in the evenings. Gary's children would not lack for aunts and uncles and grandparents' involvement in their lives, and his wife would not lack for help in the physical tasks of farm life. A good, supportive family can motivate a paralyzed person to work hard to be the best they can be amidst devastating circumstances.

Chapter Ten

The Promise

My boss Don was ahead of his time. He did things no one else was doing in the early 1970s, at least in Belleville. He saw the benefits of relaxation and meditation for patients. He developed a cardiac program for people who had suffered heart attacks or had heart surgery, in which we therapists gradually introduced exercises and got them up on their feet much quicker than previously thought good for them. Cardiac patients were normally kept lying in bed for a month or more. Don believed this was detrimental to their recovery and advocated with the doctors to get patients up and walking faster. He was a well-read man who wrote articles for the local physical therapy trade journal. I felt privileged to work under him.

One of Don's *avant-garde* ideas was to have us therapists make hospital rounds with an orthopedic surgeon named Dr. Hurd. The surgeon would discuss each postoperative patient's condition with us, then request our help in the person's recovery by saying things like, "I'd like you to take her down to PT three times a week to improve range of motion."

We were also allowed to put on masks and gloves and enter the operating room to observe orthopedic surgeries up close. That was almost unheard of in those days! I loved orthopedics because the patients got better. And, because I always saw improvement, there was little to feel depressed about. I would have been happy to stick with orthopedic surgery patients forever, but one day, Don sent me to the general medical floor. This was not an exciting assignment for a young physical therapist, but we all had to take our turn doing it. That's when I met Michael.

When I first saw Michael, I had to catch my breath because I'd rarely seen a handsomer man. Tall and slim with dark, wavy hair and a mustache, he had olive skin that hinted at Mediterranean ancestry. His eyes were the color of caramel. Immediately I felt nervous. I had a long-distance boyfriend about whom I was serious, but I wondered if I would be too distracted by Michael's good looks to focus on treating him. When my eyes fell to a gold band on the twenty-eight-year-old's left fourth finger, I breathed a sigh of relief.

"What's going on?" I asked Michael, even though I had read through his chart. He told me the doctors couldn't figure out why his legs and arms were weakening for no apparent reason. His doctor had ordered a physical therapy muscle test—a time-consuming procedure in which I would have to evaluate muscles throughout his whole body and label each one's strength as good, fair, poor, or zero.

Admittedly, I wasn't thrilled about doing the hour-long test. It would be a complicated and laborious task, and I'd have to refresh my memory on how to do it by spending my lunch hour poring over my manual muscle book. I told Michael I'd be back, and when I returned in the afternoon, he greeted me with a radiant smile. That smile melted my heart. I set about evaluating his entire body, hoping each muscle would earn the grade of "good."

As I tested Michael, I realized that he was far too thin for a man of his height. Knowing stress can cause a person to lose weight, I thought maybe he'd been worrying excessively about his condition. The gleaming wedding ring he wore spun loosely around his finger, and his belt had to be cinched to the very last hole to hold his pants up on narrow hips. His hands were not those of a manual laborer. He told me he worked a desk job for Marsh Printing, a local, family-owned company.

Belleville at that time was filled with small, family-run businesses. The quintessential small, midwestern American town, Belleville had been a lovely place to grow up. With a population of 40,000, it was small enough for its inhabitants to know almost everybody, but large enough to have a movie theater and some swanky stores and restaurants. Our town was set like a jewel in the middle of farm country. Hardwood trees like maples and oaks graced the landscape with vivid colors each fall and lush green in spring and summer. Streams and creeks that fed into the nearby Mississippi cut through the earth just outside of town in all directions.

When nothing interesting was going on in town, my friends and I got up to typical teenage shenanigans. Michael was older than me, but I wondered if he, too, had driven with his friends out to rural areas to take turns stargazing from the tops of moving cars. It was a teenage tradition in our town. One of us drove while the others lay on top of the car, facing upward. As we circled the small country roads that divided the cornfields from the soybean fields, we thought we were being wild, daring, and crazy. I guess we were, since we could have easily been thrown from the vehicles onto the asphalt and suffered serious damage. One night, we drove too fast around a curve and the car ended up in a cornfield. Thank God we were all *inside* the car on that occasion.

Danger attracted us. We stole away for secret swims in the strip mine lakes, having no idea what lay beneath the murky water filling those discontinued coal pits. How deep were they anyway? We didn't know. Were there sharp rocks underneath? Probably. Mud that could suck us down? Possibly. The strip mines were remote and the chances of getting timely help if someone ran into trouble were next to none. We thought we were living on the edge, and because we were young and stupid, we loved it!

Of course, we also had the advantage of St. Louis being just across the river. All it took to enter that exciting city was to drive ten miles west of Belleville and cross the Eads Bridge. The older we got the more St. Louis became our playground. It had museums, department stores, and lots of theater and musical events. I adored the Municipal Opera! My friends and I saw the stage production of *Pillow Talk* with Doris Day and

Rock Hudson there. All we had to do to get free seats was arrive there by three o'clock in the afternoon when it was hotter than hell. We wore hats to protect us from the sun. With lunches in hand, we sat there all afternoon, taking turns getting up to get water. Finally, at 7:30 p.m., the show would start. I happened to be at what we called the "Muny Opera" the night Neil Armstrong walked on the moon. I watched him take those steps on the TV at the concession stand.

I saw some amazing things as a teenager in St. Louis: Katharine Hepburn in *The Trojan Women* and Rudolf Nureyev in *Swan Lake* at Keil Auditorium, as well as Isaac Stern and Van Cliburn at Powell Symphony Hall. I had started riding the bus to the city with my mother as a child, but later, gangs of us teenagers would spend the day there, riding the bus across the river in the morning and taking another home at night. We shopped, went out to lunch, took in show after show after show. To us, it was a grand city! In contrast, Belleville was deadsville. Not even Belleville's bowling alley dances and street dances, in which the downtown area was closed to cars and bands set up to play, could compare to the excitement of St. Louis.

How could a little farming town compete with a big city? Belleville had been founded by German and Welsh farmers and coal miners in the 1800s. We always heard that Charles Dickens visited Belleville once, but I can't imagine why unless he stopped there on his way in or out of St. Louis. Our town did have a few nice things by the time I was growing up, but of course, in Dickens' time, the place didn't have the movie theaters we enjoyed in the 1950s and '60s. We went to the Ritz and the Lincoln constantly! I saw *Gone with the Wind* at the Lincoln Theater. We also had an orchestra—the Belleville Philharmonic.

At the time I met Michael, I was singing in the Belleville Philharmonic Choir. Michael and I talked about music; we swapped stories and laughed, and he grew so comfortable in my care that he began to speak freely to me about his condition. Michael said he'd been experiencing falls at home. He felt numbness and tingling in his hands and feet. His doctor's response was to put him in the hospital and run tests, including the whole-body muscle test I'd done on him. He'd flunked it.

I didn't tell him that right away. It wasn't my place. Michael asked me if I'd be willing to come and visit him when I had spare time, because he was bored. His wife Laura had a full-time job, and she couldn't be there all the time. He was tired of watching TV and doing crossword puzzles; he wanted human interaction with someone close to his age.

Michael's neurologist did a spinal tap and reviewed the results of the muscle test. The next time I went to his room, he said to me, his face ashen, "They think I have multiple sclerosis."

My heart sank for Michael, but the diagnosis didn't surprise me. His muscle weaknesses were all over the place, and spotty. At best, he'd tested fair, and at worst, poor. "It's what I feared all along," he confided. Then he fixed me with those caramel eyes. "Would you be my therapist through this? I don't know where this is going to end, or what's going to happen. But I trust you, and I feel I can really work with you."

I told him I would do my best to make that happen. I felt sad for Michael because I knew his prognosis wasn't good. In those days, they didn't have the drugs they now use to help people with Multiple Sclerosis. All the doctors could do for

Michael was tell him not to tire himself out, because that would only make things worse. That he would one day be confined to a wheelchair was inevitable. With all the bad news coming his way, Michael felt himself sinking, and he grabbed onto me to keep from going under.

Perhaps because Michael symbolized youth, beauty, and vitality, the thought of him ending up in a wheelchair deeply depressed me. At age twenty-one, it felt like a slap in the face. I went into Don's office and said, "This disease is going to rob Michael of his strength, his youth, and his enthusiasm. It's going to beat him down. He asked if I would be his therapist, but I probably won't be able to see him consistently."

Don assured me I could. "We can see to that," he promised. "Just remember, though, that Michael doesn't need your pity. Feeling sorry for him is not going to help him. He needs your skills, your compassion, and your support. You've got to put sorrowful emotions aside, compartmentalize them, and get to work. And don't *ever* let Michael see that you're sad for him."

That stern talk from Don led me to learn how to compartmentalize my feelings about patients. Going forward, I never took those feelings home at the end of the day. After what I'd been through with Gary and his broken femur, I knew I couldn't live under such a burden any longer. The memory of it still haunted me, but I felt determined to overcome it.

Michael didn't seem nearly as depressed as I felt. The fact that he remained positive made my job as his primary therapist so much easier. He was determined to beat the disease. I knew he couldn't beat it, but I never said so. I just enjoyed talking with him and finding things to laugh about, even amidst tragedy. I made a pledge to myself that I would never let Michael see my sadness. One can have compassion for another without shedding a tear.

Sometimes, male patients respond much better to female therapists than to men. People tend to automatically assume that a woman will be gentler and more understanding than a man. That could be what drew Michael to me, but his connection with me could also have been due to the fact that we were both young and in our twenties. He saw me as a contemporary, a hometown girl who'd lived the same teenage life he had, if seven years later.

If Michael had dark days, I didn't know about it. He kept them to himself. He was an excellent teacher to me; working with him, I learned so much about all the necessary things to teach a patient who is losing muscle strength. It felt awkward having to take Michael to the bathroom, to pull his pants down and help him onto the toilet. He made light of it, but I felt protective of his dignity. I always got out of there as quickly as I could and called for Don or Jay to take over and clean him up.

I could run away, but Michael couldn't. This was his new reality. He was deteriorating from a tall, strong, vibrant young man into a shadow of his former self, totally dependent on his family for his basic needs. In the three years I worked with him, I watched him decline. By no means was he an ideal physical therapy patient because he would only get worse and not better. Still, I was determined to help him make the most of what he had, to seize whatever shred of independence yet remained to him.

Under my tutelage, Michael learned to get on and off the toilet, how to get in and out of bed and in and out of a car. One day, when his wife, Laura, accompanied him to his appointment, I attempted to get Michael from wheelchair to car by using a sliding board. Gorgeous, dark-haired Laura stood there in a taupe, bell-bottomed Halston pantsuit and gold hoop earrings, watching me manhandle her poor husband out along the board until he slipped off and we both fell to the ground. We sat there laughing as Laura ran to fetch an aide. The big fellow picked Michael right up off the ground and plopped him back in his chair.

I felt badly about it, but Michael always had a way of making me feel better about things. He preferred to make fun of himself, saying, "There I go again. I'm such a klutz!" We practiced over and over again, until the transfer from chair to car went smoothly every time. Laura tucked him patiently into the passenger seat for the drive home, saying, "Are you comfortable, my love?" I stood there and watched her drive away, the big round diamond on her hand sparkling in the sunlight as she took the wheel. She hadn't signed up for this, but then, neither had Michael.

The next three years were not pretty. Michael went in and out of the hospital, because people with conditions like MS have respiratory issues. Each time he was admitted, he left the hospital a little bit weaker than when he'd come in. There were failed attempts to restore his bladder function. Nevertheless, I marveled at his optimism and positive nature. Having a loving spouse does wonders for a person suffering from a degenerative disease.

In the middle of those first months as Michael's therapist, my father accompanied me up to Chicago to take my board exams. I'd studied like mad for them, and was nervous, but Dad made a special occasion out of it. Even though he struggled with alcoholism, he came through for me in a big way. Always looking for an excuse to have fun, he said, "I'll go with you. Let's take the train and see the sights in Chicago while we're at it!" For a girl from a small town, Chicago was both thrilling and terrifying. Having my father with me felt reassuring and would give me the confidence to focus on the test and not on navigating a strange new city.

During the six-hour train ride, Dad smoked one Camel cigarette after another and drank gallons of coffee. While I sat in my seat, he paced up and down the aisle, looking out at the splendid farmland of Illinois. I knew he was doing his best not to drink alcohol on the trip, because I'd asked him not to. Cigarettes kept him occupied while I kept my nose in four different review books and crammed my mind with facts.

Dad had booked us a hotel near where the exams were to take place. Once we arrived and settled in, he took me out for a fancy dinner in the kind of restaurant we just didn't have in Belleville. All that evening, he drank only one martini!

The exam was brutal. It started out easy enough, with day one consisting of multiple choice and essay questions. On the second day, however, the members of the board grilled us with hard questions about how we would handle specific cases. Put on the spot, we had to answer individually, in front of everyone. That afternoon, we had a "practical exam" in which we performed treatments using various machines on volunteers from the general public. The board members watched us carefully and graded us. We also had to demonstrate a care program for a specific kind of patient, such as knee surgery, stroke, or back pain.

Illinois was known, out of all the states, to give one of the most difficult board exams for physical therapists and physicians. It was a nerve-wracking two days for me, but thankfully I passed. I had studied extremely hard throughout the four months since my graduation, and my hard work paid off.

Dad was very proud of me. He loved jazz, so we celebrated by going to a club to see Sarah Vaughn perform. We stayed in the city a couple of extra days, during which he remained on his best behavior. Apart from a few drinks at the club, he stayed away from booze for my sake. November in Chicago was cold. My ears were freezing, so Dad took me in a taxi to Macy's and bought me a hat and gloves. I called the wool, beige beanie my "good-luck hat." They must have made things well in those days because I still have it, and it's in great shape!

I told Michael all about my exam victory, and he congratulated me. He didn't even mind having such a newly licensed therapist who still had much to learn.

After three years, I married my boyfriend Jack and moved away to Arizona. I kept in touch with Don, Mickie, and

Jay for the next ten years, and they told me that Michael went to college to study technology, then took his place in the nascent computer industry. He had gone back to work in some capacity that involved his brain and not his body, although perhaps his hands were still working well enough to type on a keyboard. That was such good news to me! I pictured Laura coming to pick him up from work each evening, tucking him in, saying, "My darling, are you comfortable?" The thought made me happy.

I had promised myself to never show Michael my sadness over his condition, and I'd kept that promise. Had Michael promised himself to leave me feeling happy whenever I remembered him? If so, he'd certainly made good on it!

Chapter Eleven

The Reverend Jim

When Don assigned me to work with a certain patient one evening, I looked at the man's paperwork. When I saw what he did for a living, I panicked a bit. A pastor? Was he going to want to pray with me? Would he try to convert me to his denomination? I'd driven past his church, Winstanley Baptist, but knew nothing about it. The only pastor I'd had any contact with was the dour, unapproachable Reverend Smith at my family's Presbyterian church. I soon found out that Reverend Jim was far from being like Reverend Smith.

My boss Don was a bit *avant-garde* in that he extended our hours into the evenings a few days a week to accommodate people with nine-to-five jobs. We all took turns working those evening shifts, and I just happened to be there when Jim came in after putting in his hours at the church. He wore nice slacks with a button-down shirt and a dark sports coat. I giggled a bit when I saw that he had let the hair grow long on one side of his head and combed it over his bald pate. It wasn't a good look, but as soon as the Reverend smiled and introduced himself, I forgot all about that.

Far from being stiff and formal, as I'd imagined all ministers to be, Jim had a disarmingly friendly personality. He followed me on crutches into a cubicle and drew the curtain. I noticed his right knee was bent, and when I had him try to walk, I saw that his gait was terribly off kilter. He stepped on the ball of his right foot, resulting in an awkward limp.

"I had knee surgery three months ago," he told me, and I thought I detected a hint of sadness in his voice. "Since then, I haven't been able to straighten out my leg."

It seemed obvious to me that Jim had never had proper instruction on how to exercise his leg after the surgery. Like many patients, he probably thought if he just walked around enough, everything would go back to normal. Unfortunately, that doesn't happen. Now Jim's knee had a contracture that limited his mobility.

Dr. Hurd, the only orthopedic surgeon in town, had performed Jim's surgery, a menisectomy, trying to correct a high school sports injury that had gone untreated for decades. The surgeon had found a torn meniscus and removed it. Today, that procedure doesn't require any cutting as it's done with a scope, but back in the 1970s, it was much more invasive. After the surgery, Jim had been given the usual exercises to do, but no one was checking to see whether he'd done them correctly or often enough. That had been a big mistake which Jim was now paying for.

"My goal is to be able to walk normally when I go to the Holy Land in June," he told me. "I'm leading a group from my congregation, and it will ruin everything if I'm still limping so badly."

I had Jim lie down on the table and I measured his flexion and extension. I checked his muscle strength and the strength of his quadriceps and hip muscles. His knee range of motion was extremely limited. Because it was February and gray, ugly, and cold out, I started Jim out with moist heat packs. I placed the packs on his knee and gave him a bell to ring if he needed any help. Afterward, I did therapeutic massage on his lower thigh muscles and on the knee joint. His kneecap was frozen and wouldn't move much.

As with most knee patients, I showed him how to engage his quadricep muscles, which by then were not working well. These four thigh muscles work the knee, and if he wanted to get more leg extension, he was going to have to use them. We did quad sets, a common first exercise for anyone who has had knee surgery, and something Jim should have been doing all along. Setting a rolled-up towel under his knee, I instructed him to push down as hard as he could while tightening up the thigh muscle. At the same time, he was to lift his foot off the table.

This was nearly impossible for Jim at first, but over the weeks we worked together, we got those quads going so he could gradually get rid of the tightness and achieve more extension in his leg. Eventually, with the temporary aid of a cane, Jim re-learned to walk properly. I gave him an exercise regimen to do at home that included getting in and out of a chair several times in a row and sitting on the edge of a table with a rolled-up towel under his thigh. In this position, he was to practice lifting his leg.

In time, Jim was able to take advantage of another of Don's *avant-garde* ideas—our universal gym. This piece of machinery could accommodate up to five patients at a time, each pushing or pulling weights on pulleys. As Jim used his leg to lift weights, the other patients cheered him on. "Hey, Rev!" called out one of the guys, "Great job today! Hey, pray for me, man. I need it!"

Jim just laughed good-naturedly at that. He was so easygoing and friendly that people couldn't help but like him. He asked me questions about myself, and told me he knew of my family's business, Hill Thomas Lime and Cement. He felt certain that company had paved the driveway of his house many years before.

Over the weeks we worked together, I told Reverend Jim about my fiancé Jack, and how we were planning to get married in Belleville before moving to his hometown of Phoenix together. I confided in him that Jack wasn't a churchgoer, so we wanted to get married in my parents' home, standing before the fireplace. I asked Jim if he thought he might be able to perform our ceremony, and he said he'd be honored to do so.

When our wedding day arrived, Jack and I both had a brief meeting with Reverend Jim before the ceremony. It all went off beautifully and Jim did a wonderful job. He stayed around for the reception brunch and was there to say goodbye to us when we took off.

Jim thanked me profusely for working so hard on his knee and helping him to get better. He even wrote a beautiful letter to our hospital administrator, praising me to the skies and expressing his gratitude once again. In it, he wrote that he'd come into our PT department mildly depressed, but that when he left, his outlook was much brighter. That letter, which I still have, gave me a much-needed confidence boost as I prepared to start over again in a new city, in a new physical therapy practice.

My time with Jim solidified my conviction that working with outpatient, orthopedic patients was the right niche for me. I enjoyed seeing people's conditions improve—something that often didn't happen in neurological cases. Jim came into our department in bad shape and left in much better shape. That encouraged me greatly.

Reverend Jim was able to go to the Holy Land with his knee at about 95% of where it should have been. He sent me a postcard from there. I had truly been not only his physical therapist, but his personal trainer and cheerleader. In return, he brought a cheerful attitude and was a great listener. When a PT

works with a patient for many weeks, they can't help but get to

know each other on a more personal level. Every minute I

spent working with Reverend Jim was pure joy.

PART III

Hotter than Hell, but Healing in Phoenix

If you don't like something, change it. If you can't change it,

change your attitude.

—Maya Angelou

Chapter Twelve

The Patient in Bed Thirty-Nine

My husband Jack and I worked at two separate offices in Phoenix, both affiliated with the same practice. Mostly we saw outpatients who came to us, but doctors occasionally requested that we see some patients of theirs in a nursing home and evaluate them for physical therapy. So, on one blistering hot summer afternoon, I agreed to drive to a facility called Desert Oasis at the request of Dr. Jamison. It was the last place I wanted to go. By 4:00 p.m. each day, all I wanted to do was get in my car, blast the air conditioning, and drive to my air-conditioned home. Nursing facilities depressed me. The patients I saw there were unlikely to get well and go home. I also despised the intense heat of my husband's hometown, to which I'd agreed to move after our marriage. I longed for the gentle, humid summers of southern Illinois, with its fireflies, gurgling streams, and endless fields of corn and soybeans swaying in the breeze.

The very Memorial Day weekend of 1975 when I had married Jack, we flew to Phoenix to begin our life together. I had only ever visited Jack in his hometown in the winter, when the sun felt delightful, and the dry southwestern landscape a was a welcome change from dreary, soggy Illinois. But on our wedding day, as we exited the plane and entered the jetway, an intense heat I'd never before experienced overwhelmed me. It was so freaking hot that it knocked the breath out of me.

"It will take you about six years to get used to this," my new husband calmly informed me.

I did eventually adjust as best I could, but I relished summer visits home to Belleville. Whenever I returned to Phoenix from those visits, the city's ugly topography taunted me from below as I gazed out the airplane window. The whole area reminded me of a giant kitty litter box—brown, grainy, and generally unpleasant to look at. Summers in Phoenix made me feel like a rodent scurrying from shade to shade, circling parking lots desperate for a tree to park beneath, darting quickly from air-conditioned car to air-conditioned building lest I burn to a crisp. The temperature could soar to 122 in July. Sopping wet laundry turned bone-dry in under fifteen minutes when hung outside. Touching a car's steering wheel could burn one's fingers. The aluminum shields drivers unfold and place inside their cars' front windows didn't exist in the early 1970s, so I used to lay towels over my steering wheel and dashboard.

For better or worse, Arizona was now my home. We had good jobs in a practice that we eventually bought into, and that laid the foundation for our lifelong careers in Phoenix.

Now I drove across the inhospitable landscape of my adopted city, dreading my arrival at the nursing home. I'd never been to Desert Oasis. When I pulled into the parking lot and walked inside, I found a beautifully appointed, brightly colored reception area with chic wallpaper and shining floors. *Oh!* I thought. *This is actually a nice place.*

The lovely entrance to the place shouldn't have surprised me. A care facility's reception area often looks good, but when you make it past the doors and enter the area where the patients are kept, what a difference! I braced myself for the overpowering stench of stale urine, and sure enough, it hit me full in the face. No matter how diligently housekeeping employees mopped and scrubbed, they could never fully get rid of that smell.

I saw a couple of patients, one of whom was an elderly woman with Parkinson's who, as I walked her down the hall, urinated on my shoe. Feeling more than ready to break free of the oppressive environment and go home, I steeled myself for my last patient of the day. I found my way to a different section of the facility and said, "I'm looking for Margaret Carlson," to the nurse at the desk.

Without looking up, she pointed at the rack holding a series of aluminum folders. "You'll find her chart up there."

As I hunted for Margaret's chart, I overheard a conversation between a couple of nursing assistants.

"Did you check bed thirty-nine yet?"

"Poor thing. She'll never get any better. You should make sure number thirty-nine is turned and cleaned up before her husband gets here at 3:00."

Oh God, don't let my patient be the one in bed thirty-nine, I prayed silently. I found Margaret's chart and read, *Brain stem injury with hemiplegia and aphasia*. "This is not going to be good," I whispered under my breath. Another glance at the chart revealed that Margaret Carlson was indeed in bed thirty-nine. My next hour was going to be tough.

I cracked open the door to Margaret's dimly lit room and tiptoed toward her bed to introduce myself. The place reeked of urine. I felt sick to my stomach as my eyes adjusted and I made out the figure of a woman curled up in the fetal position. She was wide awake. Her expression reminded me of an injured wild animal backed into a corner—sheer terror. It was obvious to me that Margaret needed a bath and that she was being ignored. Pity mingled with disgust flooded me, and I felt ashamed for such an incongruous response to this patient.

Staring down at her, I was reminded of the time in childhood that my Brownie troop visited a nursing home. At the tender age of eight, I stood up before the patients slumped in wheelchairs, singing some cheerful songs and walking around greeting people. They terrified me! Even today, at age seventy-two, I have never forgotten it. It frightened me to see them immobile, some snoring, some slumped over, many of them smelling unpleasant. In 1958, adults didn't think to debrief children after such experiences. Like the other little Brownies, I took those mental images home with me and processed them in my childish mind—alone.

I was also reminded of the time when, at age twelve, I'd been enlisted to "babysit" our neighbors' bed-ridden grandmother for an evening while they went out to dinner with my parents. The wizened, white-haired woman had suffered a stroke and couldn't speak. We sat there in awkward silence, but all was well until she tried to climb out of bed and go to the bathroom. No one had prepared me for that possibility! Panicked, fearing she would fall and hurt herself, I called the restaurant. The woman's daughter immediately came home and relieved me of my onerous duties.

No longer an inexperienced child, I nevertheless had no stomach for stroke victims and their depressing prognoses. Still, I had a job to do. Margaret's insurance had run out. Her husband, a middle-income businessman, was paying for her care out of pocket and it was stretching him thin. *This is so wrong*, I thought. *This woman is not being cared for properly.* I swallowed my revulsion and put a hand on Margaret's shoulder. "Margaret, I'm Martha," I said. "I'm a physical therapist sent by Dr. Jamison."

A flicker of recognition flashed across her face at that name. She blinked and darted her eyes in my direction. I assessed Margaret as best I could as she lay there, unable to release herself from her curled-up position. Her muscles had contracted; her limbs were extremely tight. As I attempted to loosen her up and do a bit of gentle stretching, my eyes fell on a framed photograph on the table beside her bed, from which a lovely, vibrant-looking redhead in a bathing suit looked out at me. She smiled at the camera, posing by the edge of a sparkling swimming pool.

My God, is that Margaret? I thought. I paused in my work to pick up the photo and study it. *How could someone so lovely turn into this mess?* Margaret watched my every move and for all I know, she read my thoughts. Tears streamed down her face. That moment hit me full force like a boulder rolling off a cliff, straight into my heart. This was somebody's mother, wife, daughter, sister. I could not treat her as the staff treated her, with indifference. *I have a chance to change things for her*, I told myself. *I can make a difference!*

Margaret was only fifty-nine years old. The gorgeous red hair in the photograph now spread across her pillow in a tangled mess. An ugly, blue and white polka-dotted hospital gown hid her slim yet shapely figure. She looked unkempt. Her fingernails had grown too long. As my eyes traveled from her face to the photograph, I could still see the delicate features, pale skin and bright blue eyes half hidden behind her disheveled hair. She couldn't speak, but she was totally alert. She could communicate by making guttural sounds; she could smile and shake her head yes or no. With time, perhaps speech therapy could help her regain some powers of verbal communication.

"I'm here to help you," I told her. "I won't hurt you." Margaret, like so many others in her position, was completely dependent upon the whims of her caregivers. She was trapped. Her aphasia rendered her unable to speak. Often, people assume that if someone can't speak, they can't think. This is far from the truth! The alert, cognizant light in Margaret's eyes convinced me I owed her something better than what she was getting. I told her I wanted her to get better, and that together we would work on stretching out her arms and legs so that she could eventually sit up on the edge of the bed and improve her balance.

Through a slight smile, Margaret showed me that she enjoyed the sensation when I stretched her limbs. Human touch was likely in short supply at Desert Oasis. At that point in time, I had no idea whether my efforts would be rewarded with progress, but I knew I had to give Margaret my all. I was young, and I was new to that facility, so I didn't want to make waves. Yet I felt I had to speak up. I walked out to the desk and said to the head nurse, "Margaret Carlson in bed thirty-nine needs to be bathed, and she needs a fresh gown. Do you think one of the aides could do that? The patient's husband is going to be here soon."

I waited around to see what would happen. Sure enough, one of the aides bathed Margaret and changed her clothes, and just in time for her husband's arrival. Vernon, dressed in a suit and tie and fresh from the office, bent over and kissed Margaret on the cheek. Extremely attentive to his stricken wife, he touched and spoke to her tenderly. He shared the details of his day at the office with her as if they were sitting across the dinner table from one another. He told her he was going to fire up the grill over the weekend and have their kids and grandkids over for steaks and hot dogs, and that he wished she could be there. I pulled up a chair and joined him. Vernon told me that Margaret had always been an active, fun-loving woman, a real practical joker. The sudden stroke in her brainstem that had taken her down had been a shock to everyone, both inside and outside of the Carlson family.

It did my heart good to see a man so invested in his wife's care. In fact, he'd been the one to insist to Dr. Jamison that she receive physical therapy. When Vernon was ready to leave, I walked out to the parking lot with him. I'd intended to get the hell out of there much earlier, but Margaret had held me to the place like a magnet.

"I'd like to get my wife out of here and back home," said Vernon. "I know she's not getting the care she needs here. But until she's more mobile, I can't take care of her at home." He smiled wearily, and I wondered if the strands of gray in his brown hair had materialized recently, brought on by the stress of his wife's catastrophic illness.

I paused by Vernon's car and told him what I planned to do to help Margaret. "I'll work with her on sitting balance," I said. "Eventually, I hope she'll be able to get in and out of bed from her wheelchair, using a sliding board."

And that's exactly what I did. On regular visits, I took Margaret's limbs through range of motion—bending, straightening, flexing her hands up and down, working the feet and ankles so the flexor muscles wouldn't tighten up and contract. An ignored contracture will tighten up a limb so badly one can never again straighten it out. I instructed the aides to stretch her arms and legs every day, and I taught Vernon how to do the same so he could continue when Margaret went home one day.

With time, Margaret's muscles loosened up enough that she could practice sitting upright. She could shrug her shoulders and move her affected leg a little bit. However, she wouldn't be safe trying to walk unless somebody was right there with her. So, she learned to self-propel in a wheelchair down the hall, using only her good hand, for she was paralyzed on one side. With one hand turning the wheels, she could pull herself along with her good foot. I ordered a lightweight wheelchair that Vernon would be able to get in and out of the car with ease, as well as a sliding board. Walking is, of course, the ultimate goal, but when it isn't safe to do so, people can become independent in wheelchairs.

Margaret had a profound effect on me. When I met her, I was still young and didn't have much experience under my belt. Through the woman in bed thirty-nine, I realized that no matter how bleak a patient may seem, there is a person behind that crippled body. They have a soul. As a physical therapist, it is my job to help restore what dignity I can for them. In this way, Margaret served as an excellent teacher for me. I ended up needing the knowledge I gained from her, because over the years, I would see many more patients in nursing homes, and some of the cases I saw were extremely sad.

Vernon had unwittingly awakened in me the necessary compassion by placing that photograph on his wife's bedside table. The snapshot reminded me that there was a human being inside that curled up body, inspiring me to challenge others to see her as human too. We'd learned about this principle in PT training, but never had I seen it put into practice like I did that day at Desert Oasis. Ever after, I told family members to place photographs of the patient, or photographs of the patient's children, near their hospital or nursing home bed. I followed my own advice and later, when my mother was nearing the end of her life in a skilled nursing facility, I hung a framed photograph of her as a young woman above her bed. The people who came in to care for her said, "Is that Maxine? Oh, she was so beautiful!"

When my husband Jack later fought cancer and was in and out of the hospital, I always displayed pictures of our children near him. Nursing staff can easily fall into the trap of seeing a person as a number instead of a name, even as the nurses called Margaret "the one in bed thirty-nine." Unconsciously, and preoccupied with their duties, they can tend to say things like, "Get the meds for bed seventeen," or "Room twenty-four needs a bath." They should be saying, "Mrs. Jones or Mr. Smith needs a bath." Things have improved since those days, but back then, that kind of detached care could be quite dehumanizing.

Margaret did eventually go home with her loving husband, whom she was so lucky to have. Some people don't want to bring a paralyzed family member back home, feeling they can't handle it, and that they have neither the emotional nor physical capacity to care for the person. It isn't an easy task. Vernon would have his work cut out for him. Yet he so clearly wanted Margaret back home! Perhaps he had the financial means to hire in-home help on the weekdays. Thankfully, Margaret was by that time able to propel herself around her house in a wheelchair, get on and off the toilet, and in and out of bed.

I don't know what happened after Margaret went home. But I do know that patients who have loving family relationships recover faster than those who do not. There may not have been much more "recovery" in Margaret's future, but I have no doubt that her life, however, disrupted by the stroke, was full of love.

Chapter Thirteen

The Pool Hall Brawl

When a rough-looking character in leather vest and tight jeans entered my office holding the side of his face, I felt certain he'd become disoriented while looking for the dentist in our building.

"The dentist is on the third floor," I said.

"I don't need a damn dentist!" he growled. "I can't open my mouth." He handed me a prescription from the facial surgeon across the hall.

Glancing at it, I could see his name was Paul. I quickly ushered him into an exam cubicle and asked him what had happened. Paul sat down heavily, a scowl on his face. His skin was weather-beaten, his face unshaven. Dark circles ringed his eyes, as if sleep had eluded him for weeks. With his cheek swollen to outsized proportions, he resembled a chipmunk with a chip on his shoulder.

Anger oozing from every pore, he informed me that he'd been down on the south side of Phoenix one night, betting on and playing pool and having a run of good luck, winning most of the games. He'd just collected his winnings and walked out the door when two men jumped him. They accused him of cheating and demanded his money. Paul refused to hand it over, and a fight ensued.

One of the sore losers carried a pool stick. He whacked Paul hard across the face with the heavy end, and the force of the blow knocked Paul to the ground. He passed out. When he came to, he found himself in the care of paramedics who took him to the hospital, where X-rays showed his mandible and zygomatic arch were fractured.

The surgeon across the hall from my practice happened to be on call that night. He performed a successful reduction of Paul's fractures, placing wires and pins in his jaw. Now, eight weeks had passed. The wires had been removed. I asked Paul to open his mouth as far as he could. Pain etched all over his face, he struggled to do so, but could barely open it an inch and a half.

"I can't chew solid food," he moaned, "and I'm so damn sick of milkshakes and baby food."

It was hard to picture this big, tough guy reduced to eating baby food. He seemed more the beer and barbecued ribs type. The men who frequented the bars in the seedier parts of South Phoenix couldn't have been farther from the people I rubbed shoulders with in the neatly manicured suburbs where I lived with my husband. Forty-year-old Paul gave every appearance of belonging to a biker gang. He'd lost much of his hair prematurely, and what remained had grown long and scraggly. He looked like the last person I would want to meet in a dark alley or a pool hall at night. Yet here he was, having lost about ten pounds because he couldn't chew and swallow. He kept groaning and pressing his hand to his face, obviously in intense pain.

"What I need to do is work on your temporomandibular joint," I said.

"What the hell is that?"

"It's the joint responsible for opening and closing your mouth." I took measurements of how far Paul could open his mouth that day and planned to measure his progress week by week. I had him lie down on the table. "This will probably hurt a bit," I warned. Then I picked up a piece of equipment commonly used in those days—a therapeutic ultrasound machine. This deep heat device is different from the kind of ultrasound used on pregnant women. Its heyday began in the 1950s and continued through the 1980s. It's still in use today, although not nearly as often. Why this is so is a mystery to me, because it works! Therapeutic ultrasound transmits heat into the deeper tissues, warming affected muscles and joints, loosening them up and helping them to become more mobile. I pressed the ultrasound wand to Paul's jaw, moving it around the temporomandibular joint, trying to aim the heat where it needed to go.

During these seven-minute treatments, Paul couldn't feel the heat on his skin, but the meter on the machine indicated heat was penetrating the muscles of his jaw. Whenever a joint is affected, there is usually swelling, especially after surgery, so after every heat treatment, I massaged his swollen face with my hands. Then, I would have him lie on the table, where I applied moist heat packs to his jaw. All these heat treatments felt soothing to Paul and gave him hope that relief was just around the corner.

In the beginning, Paul seldom spoke except to spew out an expletive or two about how uncomfortable he was. With his attitude and menacing appearance, I would have assigned him to a male therapist if I'd had one on the premises, but my husband Jack was managing our practice's other location, so it was me or no one. With time, however, Paul softened up. He told me he was a long-haul truck driver, and that playing pool was how he'd always kicked back and relaxed when he wasn't on the road. As a divorced, single guy, he could stay out all night, drinking and betting on the games.

Now, the strong pain medication he was taking rendered him unable to drive for a living. He was bored stiff, just sitting around on disability. His jaw hurt too much to go to the bars, and he took no pleasure in eating. In short, he'd lost everything that was important to him. He felt mad at the world. The one thing that cheered him up was knowing the guy who'd hit him was now in jail because Paul had pressed charges.

Typical of many male patients of mine, Paul looked unkempt, though he didn't smell bad like some do. When they are in pain and the joy of life has disappeared, people— especially men—often let themselves go. Thinking, *What the hell, I can't even eat food or do the things I love*, Paul gave up caring how he looked. Helping a patient to move past pain and regain some mobility is to help them gain a new lease on life and motivate them to care once again about their bodies and their social lives.

I had Paul practice opening his mouth as far as he could, then close it again. I showed him how to put his hand inside his mouth and gently stretch it open. We always did this right after the heat treatments when his muscles were limbered up.

He came in three times a week for ten weeks. In those days, insurance paid for more therapy sessions than it does now. Paul spent an hour with me each time. Sometimes I administered his treatment and sometimes I had an aide do it under my supervision. By the end of six weeks, he was able to chew a little bit of meat. By the end of ten weeks, he could eat any solid food he wanted. His pain had been greatly reduced, and he was back on the road and in the bars of South Phoenix, shooting pool.

Paul's case was unique to me because never before had I seen a patient with a fractured jaw, and certainly no one with an injury resulting from an act of violence. I had to do research to even begin to know how to treat him, but I found nothing about post-fracture of the mandible. I didn't know whether ultrasound would truly help but figured it couldn't hurt to try. My success shocked me! The large, strong muscle called the masseter, which controls the opening and closing of the mouth, had contracted so tightly during the eight weeks of Paul's recovery from surgery that I knew I had to pull out all the stops and try something new. Because therapeutic ultrasound actually worked, I wrote the case up in a physical therapy trade journal so other PTs could take advantage of my experience.

I believe that deep heat ultrasound should be fully in use today. In my experience, it is effective. My patients loved getting their ultrasound treatment because they always felt better immediately afterward.

Unfortunately, today's physical therapists do not administer nearly as much hands-on treatment as we did. We were taught to take special care of our patients. Once, I had a couple of students working under me. As we escorted a patient down the hall, I noticed they kept themselves five to six feet away from the person. I said, "You know, when you're walking with a patient, you don't know if that person is going to fall. You've got to keep your hand on them and be ready in case they lose their balance." The students looked at me as if

135

I'd just landed from Mars. It seemed they'd never heard such a thing.

These days, therapists have their assistants take care of much of the one-on-one patient interaction. This is because they are hindered by insurance companies that place restrictions on their time.

Chapter Fourteen

To Amputate, or Not to Amputate

One gorgeous spring morning in Phoenix, Tony entered our practice. The moment the twenty-two-year-old man walked in, I was struck by his friendly smile and athletic appearance. Tall and slim, with a head of curly brown hair, Tony looked extremely fit. He wore a University of Arizona T-shirt and shorts. At first glance, I saw nothing amiss, and for all I knew, he could have wandered in by accident, looking for something or someone else. But alas, he was looking for me.

A closer look revealed why: Tony's dominant right arm hung limply at his side. *Oh God*, I half-thought, half-prayed. *What happened to this guy?* Surely, he couldn't have had a stroke at such a young age! He explained to me that he'd been violently thrown from his motorcycle in a collision, and that his right arm had taken the brunt of the impact. With great force his brachial plexus had been torn away from the spinal cord, severely damaging all the plexus nerves that enervated his right arm and hand.

His father, a primary care physician, had sent him everywhere possible, even to the Mayo clinic, enlisting all the best neurologists and neurosurgeons to see if they could help. They couldn't. Now, a neurologist had sent him to me in what felt like a last-ditch effort.

As we got acquainted, Tony's eyes often glanced wistfully out the window. Spring in Arizona was the perfect time to ride a motorcycle, and he remarked that he longed to be out there again, speeding down the highway. The brief interlude between drab winter and blisteringly hot summer offered an ideal opportunity to be outside with the wind in his face.

Everyone in Phoenix loves the spring. The air is heavily scented with orange blossoms. The slumbering desert, having looked so dull and brown for months, awakens into colorful life. African daisies spring up. Cacti erupt with gorgeous, delicate flowers of yellow, hot pink, deep purple, and red. We all desperately try to hang onto comfortable weather as long as possible, knowing a hot-as-hell summer looms before us. The exquisite flowers popping out of thorny cacti seem to symbolize our escape from ugly winter, even as their short-lived glory mirrors the brevity of our relief. We feel in sync with the saguaros, the hedgehog cacti, and the beavertail cacti as they stretch their limbs and blossom, if only for a couple of weeks.

"I sure do miss riding," said Tony again, his eyes continuing to wander out the window. He explained to me that he'd just graduated from college and had been accepted to medical school for the fall. He'd been celebrating with a motorcycle ride when the accident happened. He'd planned to follow in his father's footsteps and join a primary care practice. But unless he experienced what we called a "return of function" to his limp arm, that wasn't going to happen.

There was much at stake for Tony. We *had* to try. Unless a nerve is cut with a knife, and Tony's wasn't, there is always a possibility, however slight, of nerve function return. So, hoping for this, the neurologist who sent him to me ordered therapy for range of motion of Tony's entire right extremity, as well as electrical muscle stimulation.

Tony's arm, hanging useless at his side, needed to be exercised, even though it wasn't working. To help his circulation, I gave him direct current stimulation to the nerves.

Tony enjoyed it when I stretched out all the muscles of his arm, hand, and shoulder to keep them from contracting. I had him start wearing a sling to keep his arm against his body, and I ordered a forearm brace to keep his hand from becoming claw-like.

Using diagrams and detailed instructions, I explained to Tony how important it was to work his hand and arm at least twice a day so the muscles wouldn't tighten up. If some of his nerve function was to return, the muscles would need to remain flexible for him to regain use of his limb.

Only time would tell if Tony's arm could become useful again. As I worked with him three times a week, he confided in me his hopes and dreams of going to medical school and told me all about his girlfriend Chrissy. "We met in chemistry class," he said. "She loves to ride on the back of my motorcycle. Well, she *did*. We used to take off on my bike every chance we got, but I can't ride now, with only one hand working. We liked to go camping together too, but now . . . well, this arm just gets in the way of everything I try to do!"

Tony generally had a subdued expression, but his eyes brightened whenever I asked him about the things he enjoyed doing. When I attached electrodes to his arm, he could see the muscles jump, and that encouraged him. "Oh, look! My arm is moving. My fingers moved! Did you see that?" The involuntary, jerking movements gave Tony hope.

He was pleasant and easy to talk to, but his ease of conversation did little to hide an underlying sadness. I could sense that he was struggling to deal with the day-to-day challenges of learning to live life with one working arm. He had to learn to write with his left hand. When someone loses a limb, it throws the whole body off balance.

Tony's arm had no sensation, but he could feel it when I stretched it high over his head. He enjoyed that. Therapeutic touch did him a world of good emotionally. It meant someone cared about him and was doing something for a situation over which he had no control.

A year passed. Another wonderful Arizona spring arrived. Desert marigolds, brittlebush, and apricot mallow bloomed, but Tony's arm remained limp. Sadly, and not for lack of effort on my part, he experienced no return of nerve function, and the nerve conduction velocity tests run by his neurologist showed absolutely no improvement.

In what felt like a total defeat for me, Tony decided to have his arm amputated. I couldn't blame him. A limp arm just gets in the way, slows a person down, and hinders moving forward into a new paradigm. It is dead weight. During my last visit with him, Tony put up a brave front and said in as casual a voice as he could muster, "I'll just get this old thing cut off." The loss of his limb meant he no longer had the hope of a medical career. It meant a major shift in the course of his life, but he had come to accept it by then.

Eventually, Tony surely went on to be fitted with a prosthetic arm. He most likely learned to drive a car that was specially outfitted for a one-handed driver. He could do so many things—run, walk, feed himself, wash himself, operate all kinds of gadgets. The rest of his body was in top condition! Still, I felt disappointed that I hadn't been able to help him, and that his only way forward was to amputate.

Tony taught me that there were certain conditions that I as a physical therapist could do little to change. Knowing his brachial plexus was so badly injured and that his nerve conduction tests showed absolutely no return of function, I had to accept that I couldn't help every patient that came to me. I could, however, be a compassionate listener. I could be empathetic and encouraging. If all I could do was alleviate symptoms, such as Tony's arm tightening up and becoming stiff . . . well, then that was worth something.

Tony had to go through all the steps toward the ultimate acceptance of an amputation: *I went to therapy; my arm still isn't working. Martha stimulated the nerves; it still isn't working.* When he saw that I gave it my all, to no avail, he was helped on his journey to the inevitable and best choice for him. I may not have been able to reverse his condition, but I had the privilege of journeying with him for part of the way.

Chapter Fifteen

Behind Closed Doors

When my husband passed away from cancer, I became a widow with two young daughters to raise. As a single parent, I needed flexibility in my schedule so I could put my girls on the school bus in the morning and be home by the time they got off the bus. That's when I became a home health therapist. Seeing patients in their homes meant I could schedule the appointments to revolve around our family's needs.

I contracted myself out to two agencies and never lacked for work. I loved it! It's one thing to have a patient come onto my turf in an office or hospital setting, but quite another to go into someone's home and see firsthand what their daily life is like and what obstacles they may face in their recovery. Do they have a supportive person at home? Are there dogs and cats to trip over, or throw rugs lying there waiting to slip out from under them? Can they get in and out of their bathrooms? Up and down the stairs?

Safety was my number one concern. I assessed whether the patient could move around safely with a walker or cane. I looked for grab bars in the bathroom. If they didn't have any, I recommended they be installed, and I often ended up ordering a toilet chair or insert for the person. By far the worst-case scenario was when a patient did not have anyone at home to support and look out for them—at best, a loving partner or adult child; at the very least, a friend, a neighbor, someone from a church community to look in on them. In the 1990s, with no cell phones, a disabled person could get help in an emergency much more quickly if they had a partner at home.

Substance abuse often reared its ugly head in home health care. Often a nurse would come in once a week to review medication instructions with the patients, but they couldn't be there every day to monitor what that patient was doing. Many of my patients were elderly; they were on medication and some of them drank alcohol on top of it. That combination contributed to balance problems and in extreme cases caused hallucinations. One day when I entered a patient's home, he cussed me out and threw a shoe at me. I believe he was hallucinating. Half a bottle of vodka sat open on his kitchen counter right next to some strong pain medications. This man lived alone. His house was a mess. I believe he drank out of loneliness, and if he'd had a partner to watch over him and oversee his alcohol intake, that shoe might never have been launched in my direction.

Another man, a seventy-eight-year-old divorcee named Bill, had lived alone for years. He'd fallen into a common trap I witnessed over and over again in Phoenix. Younger retired people moved to Arizona for the sunshine, thinking they were moving to paradise, yet they left their children, siblings, and friends behind to do so. As time went by and they experienced health challenges, they found themselves with no support system. A son or daughter might fly in once every year, but was that enough to properly assess how an elderly parent was doing? Was a sunnier climate worth the isolation, I wondered.

I'd wrestled with that same question after Jack passed away. *Is it really worth it to stay here without a support system,* I thought, *just so I won't have to deal with dreary midwestern winters? Or should I be taking my girls and moving back to Illinois?* I knew that as long as things were going well, living in Phoenix would be fine for us. But if disaster struck in the form of a serious accident or illness, I would be in for a physical and psychological challenge. I was young and involved in a church community, so I stayed. For an elderly person with no community, however, that probably wouldn't have been the right choice.

When I entered Bill's condo, I could barely make my way down the hall through piles of old newspapers and stacks of books, boxes, and manila folders crammed with old receipts and documents. This desire to hang on to things isn't uncommon among the elderly, but Bill's place had reached the level of hoarding. The accumulated junk meant it was difficult for him to get around his own home.

Bill's place was dark and gloomy. It smelled stale and musty. Dishes encrusted with every dinner for the past two weeks sat piled in the sink. Unable to empty the overflowing trash can in the kitchen, Bill had taken to tossing his garbage into piles around the house. Dirty clothes lay in odd places. The deplorable state of his dwelling shocked me. From the outside, I never would have guessed what lay hidden behind closed doors. Bill was unable to clean up the inside, but apparently, the condo association took care of the exterior— pulling weeds, keeping the rocks raked, caring for the cacti planted here and there in patches of earth.

On my first visit to Bill, I heard a quavering voice call out, "This way! I'm back here." I found him lying in a bed, the sheets of which had probably not been changed for many weeks. The unshaven, disheveled form before me did not look like promising rehab material. Neither were these surroundings good working conditions. *What can I possibly hope to accomplish here?* I thought, already feeling defeated by the depressing environment.

My patient didn't seem embarrassed by the state of his home. Bill was so lonely that he sat up in bed and welcomed me as if I were walking into the Taj Mahal. I felt compassion for the man because I knew he didn't have any help. He'd probably managed all right before his injury, but now he'd let himself go, his face covered with many days of stubble and his clothes looking like he'd slept in them for weeks. Like so many men with serious injuries, he had lost the will to groom himself. He'd neglected bathing and changing clothes regularly. I knew that this lack of self-care could spiral down to a loss of motivation to do the necessary things to help himself get well.

After knee surgery and weeks in bed, Bill's strength had gradually wasted away. He could barely haul himself out and stand up, let alone walk. "Please, please help me," he pled. This simple question let me know that I was in business. He desired healing, and that was half the battle. We needed to get him up out of that bed, walking to the bathroom and kitchen, then eventually outside to his car so he could go places.

I opened Bill's bedroom curtains, turned on a lamp, and got to work. With daylight flooding into the condo, both our spirits lifted. Things were looking up. I planned on checking with the nurse on Bill's case to see if an aide could come to the home to help him shower. This man was highly motivated to get up and get out of his predicament! I knew a friendly face at the door a couple times a week would mean so much to him, as it does to all shut-ins who are trying to recover from physical disability.

With consistent physical therapy, Bill's condition began to improve. I merely had to focus on *him* and not his surroundings. Over the weeks, the condo's improvement did not keep pace with its owner's. It continued to look and smell unpleasant. I was there for Bill, however, and the sooner he was up and around, the sooner his living conditions would improve. And he did eventually improve enough to resume a normal life. When I finished with Bill, I felt as if I were saying goodbye to an old friend.

Doing home health visits, I saw everything from shacks on the wrong side of the tracks to palatial estates in Paradise Valley up in the hills. I saw decrepitude and disorder and gleaming homes that were spick and span from top to bottom. I saw lonely widowed and divorced people with no extended family nearby, and happily married folks with a host of caring relatives who dropped by constantly to check in.

One day I drove through two guard gates, onto the grounds of a vast, elegant home belonging to a prominent neurosurgeon in Phoenix. His mother-in-law, who lived on the premises, needed my services. The doctor's wife was always gracious and welcoming to me, but on this particular day, she was frantic.

"My car won't start!" she cried. "How am I going to get my kids to school?"

I handed her my keys. "Here, take my car," I said. "I'll be here for the next hour anyway and won't need it."

After that, we became friends. She knew I was a widow with two young daughters. We enjoyed talking whenever I came by, and she invited us to the family Christmas party. One small act of kindness resulted in a rushing waterfall of gratitude and a pleasant, casual connection that went a bit beyond physical therapy. When one sees people in their homes two to three times per week, one gets to know them. With some of them, I couldn't wait for the round of PT to end; I was more than ready to move on. With others, I hated to see my visits draw to a close. The hospitable ones invited me to have coffee or tea with them at their kitchen tables. They offered me food. I usually declined food, but there were times I missed my lunch break, and a muffin or sandwich was more than welcome to keep me going through the day.

One day, I showed up at the home of a seventy-three-year-old woman with a history of falls. I knocked on the front door of the tidy little ranch-style home in a Phoenix suburb and a diminutive, white-haired woman answered. She wore her hair in a tight bun. I knew my patient had suffered a spinal fracture at T11 due to osteoporosis and had become debilitated because of the pain, so it shocked me to see her up and around, wearing an apron. Such fractures are seen mostly in women because of the loss of estrogen as they age.

"Are you Mrs. Williams?" I asked. "I'm surprised to see you up and around!"

She looked up at me with bright, blue eyes. "Well, I *am* Mrs. Williams, but I'm not your patient. Come on in. It's my daughter-in-law you're wanting to see."

The elder Mrs. Williams led me to a bedroom. "I'm doin' the nursin' around here," she said, and pointed to a woman lying in bed. "That's my daughter-in-law, Sharon."

Sharon smiled up at me. "My mother-in-law Alice is ninety-seven," she said, "and she takes care of all of us." After Alice left the room, Sharon whispered, "I let her nurse me because it makes her feel good." She continued, "Mom can't hear well. She needs glasses to read the paper with her one good eye."

As I evaluated Sharon, I could see Alice through the open bedroom door, frosting a cake for her seventy-three-year-old son's birthday. She reminded me of a bird, the way she hopped around the kitchen, wearing wire-rim glasses and little white socks with slip-on flats, never sitting still, her hands constantly busy. Her sharp features stood out all the more for her being so thin. She'd baked muffins earlier that morning. Now she offered me one and made me a cup of coffee. Because my schedule was somewhat flexible that day, I sat down to enjoy the treat. I asked Alice about her family. She told me her parents had come out West on a wagon train.

"I have ten children, thirty-four grandchildren, forty-five great-grandchildren, and a handful of great-great-grandchildren," she replied. "Among them, there's always somebody that needs my help, and that's what makes me happy." When asked her secret to living such a long and energetic life, she said, "It's simple. I never sit down. I'm always moving, always on my feet."

Overhearing our conversation, Sharon called out from the bedroom, "Mom eats her meals standing up. She works all day, and then just collapses into bed at night."

Surely that was an exaggeration, but probably not much of one. As a devout Mormon, Alice must have sat still in church on Sundays. She probably relaxed long enough to watch the news on television or read the newspaper now and then.

But she also probably jumped right back up afterward and got back to work.

As she told me of her active lifestyle, a Robert Frost poem popped into my mind, and I thought, *This woman has miles to go before she sleeps.* She'd definitely done *something* right. Alice had never had cancer, or a stroke, or any of the other maladies that afflict the elderly. I knew there was truth to her philosophy. It is much better to be on one's feet and moving around. Sitting is the new smoking. Sitting in front of a computer all day, as many people must do for their jobs in this day and age, is not good for one's circulation. It is not good for the bones. It is being up, walking around, that keeps bones strong. And weight-bearing exercise—carrying sacks of groceries home from the store, doing exercises with weights, walking with a five-pound weight in a backpack—builds bone mass.

Alice was not shy about sharing her prescription for a long life: "I never used tobacco or liquor, but I drank lots of strong coffee up until a few years ago when my doctor made me quit. He said it was bad for my heart. I was never afraid of hard work, like picking cotton. I did that as a child. I always kept my hands busy and my feet moving."

I could plainly see that Alice's gnarled hands were arthritic, but she didn't seem to focus on that at all. She probably relied on anti-inflammatory medication to keep her going, along with the fact that among her large family, there was always someone having a baby or recovering from an illness who needed her help. Here she was, nursing someone twenty-four years younger than her, and loving it!

Sharon's condition improved. Over the weeks, I got her up out of bed and put her in a brace. Then we'd go for a walk around the block. As she grew stronger, we walked outside on the sidewalk. Through the stages of her recovery, I recorded her progress in my notes: *This patient requires "stand-by assistance,"* meaning I needed to stay close by her side to ensure her safety. Eventually, she graduated to simply needing "assistance." The home health patients who needed "maximum assistance" were reserved for male PTs who were far stronger than I, for they needed to be hauled out of bed and set in wheelchairs.

As they slowly improved, I always advised patients like Bill and Sharon to get dressed each day, even if they still spent a significant amount of time resting. The sooner one gets out of one's pajamas, the sooner they feel like a human being again. Going around the house in PJs is not conducive to getting better emotionally and physically. "Get up, get dressed, sit on the edge of your bed or in a chair as if you are ready to greet visitors," I admonished my patients. "Wearing a nightgown all day will make you feel like an invalid. It promotes a mindset of 'Oh, I'm sick; I can't do anything.'"

Not that I was cavalier about my patients' discomfort! As a general rule, people with chronic back pain had the most challenging, difficult time recovering from their injuries and surgeries. Back problems affect everything one does. A person never knows whether their back is hurting because they did too much exercise or too little. I never labeled patients with chronic neck or back issues as malingerers. If they told me they were in pain, I took it as the truth.

Over my forty-year career, I observed that those who were chronically overweight had greater difficulty recovering from injuries and illnesses than slimmer, more active people. If someone has neglected their health and can barely walk around the block, that doesn't bode well for recovery. Yet there are other factors that contribute to a poor recovery. Sometimes, I walked into homes in which I immediately sensed unhappiness and a palpable tension between caregiver and patient. Caregivers can experience burnout. They become mentally and physically exhausted.

One patient I worked with was a retiree who had moved from Michigan to Phoenix with his wife to live in a sunnier climate. Chronically overweight, Vic had let himself get out of shape by spending lots of time in front of the TV and eating junk food. Because he was tall and weighed around 265 pounds, his wife Judy had trouble caring for him after he had back surgery. Unable to get out of the house much, he became cranky and critical. Judy longed to get out more with her friends, but Vic felt lost without her and made a fuss every time she wanted to go shopping or out to lunch. He was no longer the kind man she'd married.

Judy desperately needed relief but all their family members, including their children and Vic's brothers, lived far away and were unable to come over and give her a break. She felt trapped. So did Vic. Judy's resentment built up even as Vic

continued to take out his frustrations on her. Alcohol

consumption fueled the arguments between them. I was always

relieved when it was time to leave their home after a visit, but I

felt terribly sorry for Judy being stuck at home with a grumpy

old man in a town in which they had no support system.

Chapter Sixteen

I'll Never Smile Again

Nadine walked into my office resembling a movie star from the 1950s. She looked at me through the dark lenses of oversized designer sunglasses and adjusted the long silk scarf draped over her head, as if she wanted it to hide more of her face. The woman seemed agitated.

From Nadine's paperwork, I already knew she had Bell's palsy. Still, I wasn't prepared for what I saw when she reluctantly pulled the scarf from her head. This relatively young, elegant, refined woman, whose photograph I had seen in the society section of the local newspaper, looked like a stroke victim. One half of her face was paralyzed. Her shapely lips, which she had valiantly covered with lipstick to try to keep up some semblance of normalcy, drooped dramatically on one side.

A well-known socialite married to a prominent attorney, Nadine had smiled for many a camera over the years. Now, she could no longer smile. When she tried, the left side of her mouth refused to cooperate.

I hid my shock as I examined her face. The patch she wore over her left eye was unbecoming, yet necessary to keep debris out because Nadine could not blink.

Compounding her frustration was the mysterious nature of her predicament. Medical experts differed in opinion as to what caused Bell's palsy, a rare condition that causes sudden weakness of facial muscles. Various theories floated around. One said people caught it by riding in a car with the window rolled down and exposing themselves to the cold wind. Other weird ideas abounded, but gradually experts settled on the strong possibility the condition arose from either an infection or virus.

Ultimately, Nadine cared less about where the palsy came from, and more about what could be done to heal it. Her life took place mostly in the public eye, and now she'd had to retreat from view. She felt embarrassed. "I don't want anyone to see me like this," she said. "I'm afraid I'll never smile again!"

Doctors had prescribed oral steroids in hopes they would help the affected facial nerve, but there had been no overnight cure that would enable Nadine to again feel good about her appearance. I could see she'd done her best to present herself as normally as possible. Her hair was perfectly colored and cut, and on both hands, she wore diamond rings of substantial size and sparkle. I caught sight of the name Gucci on the clasp of her purse and had no doubt it was the real thing, probably purchased on a vacation in Paris or Rome.

That is not to say that Nadine was shallow and materialistic. She and her attorney husband may have hobnobbed with the country club set and were often seen at the finest restaurants, but I knew from the newspapers that they were also involved in many a humanitarian effort in Phoenix, donating money and helping raise awareness for a whole array of social issues. She wanted to get back to the life she found rewarding. Nadine wanted to stand at her husband's side again, without shrinking back in embarrassment.

Bell's palsy is not a permanent condition, but just how long it will take to recede after attacking someone is open to anyone's guess. A full recovery can take anywhere from three weeks to nine months. Compared to a more severe disease, that prognosis sounds fabulous, but that was little comfort to a woman whose busy lifestyle had been halted. I had to remind myself that to a woman whose life revolved around being beautiful and being seen, as well as hanging out with other beautiful people, even a few weeks of disfigurement was devastating.

Removing Nadine's eye patch, I attached electrodes to the left side of her face. Her doctor had ordered direct current stimulation to enervate the facial nerve, which in turn would make the facial muscles jump and contract. This wasn't going to contribute to Nadine's healing, but it could increase circulation to the area and make her feel a little better.

I showed Nadine exercises she could do at home to move her facial muscles. Because a functioning body part, such as the eye, can transfer some electrical impulses to the affected area, I had Nadine practice opening and closing both eyes. Even though she had no control over the paralyzed left eye, I hoped that by exercising her right eye, transference might occur. The same went for smiling. I urged her to smile routinely, even though one half of her mouth wouldn't cooperate.

Realistically, there wasn't much that physical therapy could do for Nadine except to prevent her inactive muscles from permanently contracting. I had her practice drinking out of a straw, knowing the crossover of muscle fibers and nerve impulses could help to keep the affected side of her mouth from atrophying.

I taught Nadine how to massage her face a couple times a day with lotion, including her forehead, because she could not lift her left eyebrow. This would at least keep the muscles somewhat loosened up. And because her lymphatic system on the left side was affected, massage could help to remove fluid from her face, so she wouldn't develop edema—a buildup of liquid and its resultant swelling.

Ultimately, Nadine just had to wait until the palsy went away on its own. The nerve stimulation we gave her, along with heat treatments and massage, served to encourage her. Physical touch helps people. It gives them hope. It reassures them that someone has taken note of their pain and frustration and is at least trying to do something about it. She came to me twice a week for one month. During that time, I saw no progress, but even as I said goodbye to her after the last treatment, I felt hopeful that she would recover, because I knew the virus was not permanent.

As with all neurological patients, I felt frustrated by Nadine's condition. Neurological problems were always my least favorite to work with because the outcomes were dubious. Nerves heal slowly if at all. Nerve damage is the most difficult challenge for a physical therapist. My duty, however, was to remain upbeat and positive when treating my patients. I strove to listen well and have a compassionate heart. In this, we have much more impact on a patient's emotional well-being than doctors.

Generally, physicians walk into a room, talk briefly with a patient, then walk out again. Because physical therapists spend more time in a patient's company, we provide the emotional care so often lacking today in patient-doctor encounters. We listen to them vent. They tell us their life stories, sharing their triumphs and heartbreaks. We put our hands on them, providing therapeutic touch. I found this was often the best thing I could do for a patient during my thirty minutes to an hour with them, perhaps even more important than the exercise, heat, and massage I provided. When a patient left my office, I knew they felt heard and seen. We physical therapists sought to provide physical, mental, and emotional

relief.

Chapter Seventeen

Get Me Home to Show Low

Once again, I received a call I dreaded. Another patient awaited me in a depressing nursing home on one of the hottest days of the year in Phoenix. The last thing I wanted to do was abandon my air-conditioned office on my lunch break, but I knew from previous experience that I would never regret hauling myself out there. Often, the most discouraging cases blessed me the most.

Sherri was only in her early fifties, but severe rheumatoid arthritis had crippled her and prematurely ended her nursing career. When I walked into her room at the nursing home, I found a frail, petite thing curled up on the bed. Fear radiated from her eyes. In intense pain, terrified that I would hurt her, Sherri shrank back visibly from my touch. "Sometimes the people here handle me roughly," she said in a small voice.

I held off with my examination; instead I grabbed a chair and sat down beside her bed. "I promise not to hurt you,"

I said in the calmest tone I could muster. "I just want to find out more about what I can do to help you."

In bits and pieces, Sherri confided in me that all she longed for was to get out of the nursing home and back to her trailer in the little town of Show Low in the Arizona hill country. Her hometown was named after a card game played during the era of the Wild West. When she told me of her longing to get back there, I couldn't blame her one bit. Who *wouldn't* prefer to be in the forested hills rather than ugly, brown Phoenix? Who wouldn't prefer to be in their own home rather than in a care facility?

At first glance, Sherri's case did not look promising. Her potential for rehabilitation seemed minimal, and when I read her chart, I thought, *I don't know if I'm going to be able to make a difference in this woman's life. What can I possibly do for someone with a chronic inflammatory disorder like rheumatoid arthritis?* I despaired of her ever getting out of that nursing home.

Sherri had spent her career taking care of other people, and lying in bed, helpless, felt humiliating and degrading to her. Rheumatoid arthritis ravages a person's body. Sherri had been prescribed bed rest, but the conundrum is that while bed rest does allow a person in pain to take it easy, it also causes that person to grow weaker. That's why Sherri ended up in Phoenix in a nursing home—she'd grown weak. The doctors in Show Low didn't know what to do for her.

Divorced with no children, Sherri lived alone with no one to take care of her. In her circumstances, the doctors did what they thought best for Sherri, and that was send her off to Phoenix, where a niece of hers lived and where there were plenty of nursing homes in which she could be cared for. Unfortunately, this solution only resulted in physical decline and depression.

My heart went out to Sherri. It was hotter than blazes in Phoenix and anyone used to dwelling up in the pines would surely think they'd died and gone to hell. I determined that I would do everything possible to help get her out of the city and back up into the hills. But when push came to shove, would her determination match my own? Sherri's recovery was going to be an arduous process. It would hurt like hell.

"Sherri, if you're absolutely determined to work on this with me, I'm willing to come here on my lunch hour two to three days a week. Your success will depend on if you follow my instructions, even on the days I'm not here. Are you with me?"

"I'm with you," she promised. We were going to do this!

It was a slow process, as I knew it would be. Every muscle in Sherri's body had tightened from underuse. She'd been on bed rest way too long, so she had lost many of the essential movements one needs to be able to get up and take care of oneself, and to get in a car and drive. Slowly and gently, I worked with her, teaching her how to do certain exercises on the days I couldn't be with her. We practiced movements most people take for granted—bending and straightening her elbows, raising her arms to get her shoulders moving, putting her hands behind her head.

I hunted around in the equipment closet at the nursing home and found a cane to help her increase her shoulder motion. I had her hold the cane with two hands, raise it up off her tummy as high as she could go, then bring it down again, over and over again. When we started, Sherri could hardly raise it up at all. Little by little, with lots of determination, she was able to raise it higher and higher.

We worked on her knees and hips, to increase her range of motion. In what we call "active assistive range of motion," I held onto her foot and knee and gradually, with my help, her voluntary movements increased measurably. It wasn't easy. Her muscles had atrophied, and that was no surprise. When moving the limbs increases a person's pain, it is tempting for them to just stop moving. This doesn't help them in the long run. They must work through the pain and get the movement going, and that's what Sherri and I did together. She didn't have the strength initially to raise her leg up off the bed on her own, but with me repeatedly supporting her leg as she raised it, she gradually grew stronger. I had her lie on her back and bend each knee, one at a time, then lift her toes and drag her heel back toward her bottom, then push it back down. Up and down, up and down. The bed supported her foot as she executed this important movement.

As I always did with patients, I made Sherri promise to put on regular clothes, socks, and shoes, and start thinking about *not* being a patient. I wanted her to imagine herself feeling more "human" again. Because she so desperately wanted to go home, I said, "Would you walk around your home in a hospital gown? Of course not! If you're dressed, you're more engaged in life; you are up doing things, ready for a visitor, ready to take life head on."

Sherri took my words to heart. She got dressed each day, and with time, she progressed from needing active assistance to doing all her exercises by herself. She gradually improved over the weeks and months until she was well enough to come to my office as an outpatient, riding a shuttle provided by the nursing home. How encouraging it was for her to get out of that depressing environment! She loved every minute away from there. At first, she came to me in a wheelchair. I had the privilege of watching her get up out of the chair and take her first steps, and that was exciting for both of us. She started out with a walker, then graduated to a cane.

Soon, Sherri was ready to go to live with her niece in Phoenix for a while, until she could go back to Show Low. It was incredibly rewarding for me to assist a patient in going from being bed-ridden and terrified, to upright, walking, and confident. What a fantastic outcome for a case that at first glance appeared to be hopeless! Eventually, Sherri transitioned to living independently again in her trailer in the hills.

She came to say goodbye to me before taking off for Show Low in the fall. Dressed in jeans, T-shirt, denim jacket, and cowboy boots, she thanked me profusely for getting her out of there and back up to her home. Her short hair had been cut into a neat, tidy style, and she even wore some silver filigree hoop earrings—the first time I had ever seen her put on jewelry. She did not resemble in the slightest the woman I had first encountered in the nursing home.

Sherri thanked me, but it was I who needed to thank *her*. I came away from her case with an understanding that things are not always what they appear to be on the surface. The outcome could be bad or good, but one has to scratch the surface to find out which it will be. Sherri had appeared totally compromised, in a debilitating, hopeless environment. With some patience, compassion, and listening, I learned she was not nearly as compromised as I'd thought.

Her case looked terrible on paper, but I had a real human being on my hands who was telling me she wanted more than anything to go home. What was I going to do? Trust the paperwork over a person? No. I knew I had to try to help her achieve her goal. I also knew it would be a long, drawn-out, step-by-step process, and I accepted that. In the end, it was totally worth it. Seeing Sherri transformed from that tiny, frightened, curled-up form into a confident woman on her way home felt like a remarkable and unforgettable victory to me.

Chapter Eighteen

The Great Unwashed

Nate came into my office with lower back and neck pain. These were typical complaints for young men like him, who worked in construction, slinging around building supplies and large power tools and operating heavy machinery. At thirty years old, he walked slowly, with one hand on his back to provide pressure to the aching muscles. He was a nice-looking guy who carried around a few extra pounds and had a perpetual tan from working outdoors. My heart went out to him when I saw him wince as he sat down in the waiting room. He was far too young to continue suffering in this way, so I wanted to do everything I could to give him relief. There was just one problem.

Nate stank.

Badly.

My assistant Melissa put him in a cubicle and got him set up with heat before I went in to treat him. She told him to change out of his jeans, then handed him some shorts to put on so he could more easily do exercises after ultrasound and

174

massage. Melissa left him to change and made a beeline for my office.

"I just want to let you know that there is a *very* bad odor in there," she said in a low voice. "It's a kind of sweat and unwashed body smell. A stench, really."

It was high summer in Phoenix. We were used to sweat; it was a part of our everyday lives. But sweaty is different from severe body odor resulting from lack of personal hygiene. I knew if Melissa was complaining, this was not going to be good. Dreading walking into that room, I bucked myself up with an internal pep talk. *He's your patient, Martha. You have to go in there; you have a responsibility toward him.*

I walked into the cubicle, and it was *bad.* Because we physical therapists had such hands-on contact with our patients forty and fifty years ago, I had to therapeutically massage Nate's lower back for several minutes, kneading the muscles down close to the buttocks, for his pain was at L4-5 and S1. Holding my breath as much as possible, I nearly went faint. I felt like gagging. I did the ultrasound and finished our session in record time because I just could not wait to get out of that enclosed space.

Since Nate was scheduled to come in twice a week for the next few months, I knew I had to do something about the situation. But what? I wasn't sure what the root of the problem was. I scoured his medical records but found no hint of a physical condition that could cause terrible body odor. Did Nate just not shower or bathe? From across the room, I'd seen no signs of dirt, but when I wiped down his sore area with rubbing alcohol, as I did for all my patients, the white towel removed a visible layer of grime. This puzzled me. According to his chart, Nate lived at an address in a respectable neighborhood, and he certainly didn't look like an unhoused person with no access to running water. He was friendly, polite, and comported himself with dignity. Nate was aware of all the proper social graces, yet unaware of his overpowering stench. As far as I could tell, the problem was simply due to poor hygiene habits.

Nate was unmarried and probably lived alone because a roommate or romantic partner would surely have pointed out this problem to him. It occurred to me that he may have come to our office directly from working outside in the heat without stopping to shower first. Yet, the strong smell he exuded could not possibly be the result of one day's work in the Phoenix sun. It had to be the accumulation of many days' buildup of perspiration with no washing whatsoever.

Far more important than figuring out what caused Nate's overpowering smell was figuring out what to do about it. I wanted to continue taking care of this man, but if that was going to happen, something had to give. I couldn't expect my staff to deal with it, and I just plain did not want to deal with it, so I was going to have to figure out a way to get him to bathe before coming in the next time. *But how do I approach that?* I wondered. Never before had I faced such a dilemma!

The next time Nate came in, I sat him down and delivered a speech I had rehearsed over and over in my head. In a friendly tone, I said, "Nate, this is really hard for me to talk about. You are such a nice guy, and we so appreciate that your doctor sent you here for therapy. But there's just one little problem. I know it's terribly hot outside, and these cubicles are small. There seems to be a strange odor when you're here, and I'm not sure if it's because of your job being outside in the hot sun." I proceeded to tell him that he needed to shower before he came to see us, because we had to work in a small, confined space, with doors closed for patient privacy.

I'd prepared myself for the worst, knowing there was a chance Nate would walk out, offended, and never come back. The last thing I wanted was to gain a reputation as a PT who offended her patients! However, Nate took it very well. He apologized, saying he sometimes got so busy he forgot to shower. He confirmed my suspicion that there was no one else at home to tell him when he began to smell ripe, and he promised to do better. The following week, Nate showed up for his appointment all cleaned up. He'd even splashed some aftershave on! I decided to positively reinforce this new development.

"Oh, Nate! Wow, do you smell great!" I exclaimed. "I sure love that aftershave!"

Never again did Nate appear in my office smelling terrible.

Today, it's likely to be an aide and not a therapist who bears the brunt of a smelly patient. Even a physician, who walks into a room, talks to a patient for ten minutes, then leaves, can brush off an unpleasant odor. But in the 1970s and

1980s, physical therapy was a hands-on job for the therapist, and we often spent as much as an hour confined in a small, confined space with a patient. Overpowering smells were a very real issue to us, and we had to come up with strategies to deal with the problem whenever it arose.

For instance, we often worked with people's feet. If they had ankle or foot problems, their socks came off and we had to not only massage and apply heat or ice, but we had to place the person's foot in the crook of our arm or on our forearm to stretch it, practically having their foot in our face. In our office, we came up with protocols for this. We made it our policy to, before ever putting our hands on people's feet, pour rubbing alcohol on the injured foot and wipe it down. It felt good for the patient while simultaneously removing dirt, grime, and odors. I always dried carefully between their toes. Oftentimes, the white towel would come away brown. That alcohol took care of stinky, sweaty feet, and because we did it to everyone, it caused no embarrassment to those with offending feet. For the worst cases, we used a footbath and let the patient soak in soapy water for a while before treating them.

Nate's problem was extreme, but it was not an isolated case. Because I dealt with people's bodies all day long, bad odors were often part of the equation. I owed offenders no less than direct, compassionate honesty. Sometimes, if they were elderly and suffering from dementia, there wasn't going to be much in the way of results. But I like to think that through confronting Nate forthrightly about his body odor, I helped him become more aware of how he presented to others, and it gives me great satisfaction to think I may have launched him into a more successful social life!

Chapter Nineteen

I Know It Hurts, But Keep Beating Your Stump

Fifty years ago, artificial limbs were a far cry from what they are today. Professor "Mack" MacDougal, the director of the PT program at the University of Kentucky, had a special interest in prosthetics and through him I came to learn much about them. Back then, they were heavy and cumbersome. They caused amputees great pain in their stumps, whether AK (above the knee) or BK (below the knee.) Mack taught us to prepare patients for the inevitable misery of learning to wear an artificial limb by doing something that at first sounded to me counterintuitive and cruel.

"Teach them to beat their stump with a rolled-up magazine," he said.

This was necessary, he insisted, to get a person ready for the painful reality of strapping on a heavy piece of plastic. An artificial limb was going to assault the nerve endings that remained at the end of the stump of an amputated arm or leg. The patient was just going to have to suck it up and get on with things.

So, dutifully, whenever I had an amputee as a patient, I taught them to take a magazine—a reasonably thick one, not a skinny, wimpy one—and roll it up, then slowly but gradually, with increasing force, whack the end of their stump with it. "It's going to hurt," I told them, "but it's going to help you get used to wearing your artificial limb, because your stump has to be pushed down inside the socket of that plastic limb."

When I did my amputee rotation in our clinic at the University of Kentucky, I became used to seeing four or five amputees lying on tables, all whacking their stumps. It hurt them like hell at first! But I saw firsthand how it helped to toughen up the tip of the stump so it could accept a prosthetic limb. Not even a stump sock could protect the nerves and skin from the brutality of being shoved into a hard, unyielding prosthesis, especially if it were an artificial leg and the person had to learn to walk in it.

We taught the amputees how to exercise their stumps, moving them up and down, back and forth. We used our hands to give resistive exercise as they worked what remained of their amputated limb. A patient would lay on their back or stomach, pushing their leg stump against the pressure of my hand to increase the strength of hip abduction. Then, they would lift their stump in the air and push against my hand to increase the strength of their hip flexors. Next, I had them turn onto their tummies and lift the stump behind them. That stump had to grow strong, because it was going to control everything the person did with the prosthetic limb.

A patient had a much better chance of consistently using a prosthetic leg device if their amputation was below the knee. In that case, it was far easier to control the prosthesis. A person with an above-the-knee amputation had to work extremely hard to learn to walk with the new limb, because it was so heavy. We dealt mostly with artificial legs. Upper extremity amputations were rarer, and usually the result of a congenital deformity or a violent injury.

In those days, expensive prostheses often ended up sitting in the back of an amputee's closet. These people didn't need or want intense pain on top of their already frustrating predicament. It was so much trouble to get them on and learn how to use them. Many of the patients who discarded their artificial limbs were over sixty and felt they were too old to learn the "new trick" of dealing with it. They'd lost limbs to diabetes or blood poisoning and preferred to use a walker and hop around the house on one foot rather than go through the agony of learning to wear a cumbersome piece of plastic. Young patients fared better. They often had a can-do spirit and felt motivated to adjust, because their ability to do so would affect the rest of their lives.

Maybe amputees don't beat their stumps anymore. Prosthetics have evolved over the decades and are probably much more comfortable to wear these days. They are now made of much lighter materials. Today, you might not even be able to tell that someone has a prosthetic limb if they have long pants on. They are made to fit precisely, with measurements made over time to accommodate the stump's reduction in swelling. The dedicated work of many experts goes into the making of each and every individualized prosthesis. Today, they are highly individualized, fine-tuned works of art!

PART IV

If It's Physical, It's Therapy:

Across Visible and Invisible Borders

I've learned that making a living is not the same thing as making a life. People will forget what you said, people will forget what you did. But people will never forget how you made them feel.

—Maya Angelou

Chapter Twenty

One Billion Fly Swatters

"Oh Jack, you've got to try this." I said to my husband, who sat across from me at the banquet table. "It's crunchy and tastes good!" By now, I was growing tired of wok-fried greens and other vegetables over rice, which we'd been served nearly every day during our three-week trip to communist China. I'd given up my beloved coffee for three weeks and was sick of the ubiquitous Chinese tea. I was more than ready to eat and drink something different, so tasting this savory morsel brought me great pleasure.

Jack, who'd grown up in Arizona as the son of Chinese immigrants, turned to the man sitting next to him and casually asked what I was eating. The fellow answered in Chinese, and Jack turned back to me. "Those are whole, deep-fried baby sparrows."

Oh my god! I thought, barely able to keep from gagging. I grabbed a napkin and, pretending to wipe my mouth, quickly spit the "morsel" into it. Had the bird's tiny bones and beak given it that delightful crunch? I barely made it through the rest of the meal without vomiting, which was a shame, since this banquet was our hosts' way of thanking us for the time we had spent in China. Nothing even remotely edible was wasted in those days. Certain foods were out of reach. Not once were we served beef. We ate only scant amounts of pork, chicken, and fish, and large amounts of vegetables and white rice. Unlike the average Chinese citizen in the early 1980s, athletes whose sports were subsidized by the government got plenty to eat, as did members of the Communist Party.

Because of my husband Jack's Chinese heritage, it made perfect sense for us to join the third annual Sino-American study tour to the People's Republic of China in 1981, sponsored by the American Physical Therapy Association. All twenty-five of us on the trip were eager to learn how physical therapy was practiced in China. In Beijing, Shanghai, and Guangzhou, we toured hospitals and traded information with doctors and physical therapists, observing their practices and explaining ours.

In 1981, communist China was still a relatively closed country, only in the beginning stages of opening up to visits from foreigners. The gigantic international airport at which we landed was practically empty, because few people were coming and going. The average Chinese citizen did not have permission to travel outside China's borders.

Most of the people we saw still wore the grayish blue, padded "Mao suits," but now and then, we caught sight of a Chinese person in regular clothing. The children were dressed less drably than their parents. Bright-eyed schoolchildren skipped along sidewalks in their uniforms, bright red scarves tied around their necks.

To our surprise, we learned that China had no physical therapists as we knew them in America. Instead, "doctors of physical medicine" treated patients in need of relief from physical pain due to accidents or other issues. These men and women were trained in western methods but also in traditional Chinese medicine, which meant they prescribed herbs and compounds made from bamboo extract and such strange-sounding ingredients as dried toads, seahorses, lizards, and snakes. All these things were part of a centuries-old discipline and still highly valued in the late twentieth century, as they are even today.

After being escorted to our first lodgings in Beijing, we visited the First Affiliated Hospital of the Beijing Medical College, where we were informed the sprawling place had 1000 beds and a staff of 2000. We all looked at each other incredulously, asking, "Twice as many staff as patients?"

"Yes," replied our hosts. "Everyone here in China is given a job." We soon observed that this was true. A person's job might be to trim grass or pick up trash on the street—and this was surely the reason Chinese cities were so pristinely clean and we saw no litter on the ground—or dust hospital rooms daily. But it was imperative that everyone be kept busy. All employment was useful and meaningful. We had to admire that.

China's economy in the early 1980s was nothing like it is today. Few people, probably only high-ranking members of the Communist Party, owned cars. Instead, millions of bicycles rolled through the streets. The pollution that plagues China today comes primarily from cars and factories, but back then, the pollution came from the coal people burned to keep warm in the winter.

We further learned that the facility, with its 300 staff doctors, saw an average of 3500 outpatients per day, as opposed to the 100 people seen on a busy day by a large hospital in America.

The Chinese therapists thought we were all doctors and were shocked to learn that wasn't so. We learned fascinating things from them; they told us their number one health problem during the winter months was Colles fracture—a broken wrist. It seemed those millions of bicycles slipped on icy roads and riders put their hands out to break their falls.

As we walked the halls of various hospitals in the cities we visited, we saw hundreds of people jammed into waiting areas. Medical workers moved among them, giving acupuncture treatments right where they stood. Either sitting on the floor or standing when all the seats were taken, these people in pain happily received the tiny needles administered by clinicians. These acupuncturists patiently went from one patient to the next, hour after hour, all day long. When we visited an actual acupuncture clinic, we found it to be more crowded than any other medical practice because the Chinese people trusted this traditional treatment as much as they trusted traditional herbal medicines.

In Guangzhou, at an inpatient facility for people with mental health problems, we learned from our guide that the monotony of certain jobs, such as factory assembly lines, caused mental breakdown in some people. Long separations from family members contributed to this, for many people worked in factories away from home and lived in dormitories. Among the Chinese, there were plenty of people with the intelligence to be a doctor or an engineer, but since space in universities was limited and the competition fierce to get in, they often ended up having to do for a living whatever the Communist Party told them to do. If that was tightening screws in an appliance factory for fourteen hours a day, then so be it! Such a person had little recourse.

It heartened us to see that the patients in the mental facility were well cared for. When we arrived early in the morning, we saw close to 1000 people standing out in the yard, doing Tai Chi and group exercises. As in regular medical facilities, their nurses made rounds, dispensing herbal tinctures. No hospital, whether for mental or physical patients, provided the all-important black tea to drink. Family members were expected to bring that in for their loved ones, and most patients had a large thermos by their bed, provided for them by relatives.

The mental facility fascinated us, but we were really there to learn how therapists and doctors in China treated the same kinds of patients we routinely saw—stroke patients, amputations, and all kinds of injuries. We noticed they were doing a combination of Western medicine and traditional Chinese medicine, with the Western medicine making up only a small part. Wisely, they believed exercise to be extremely important and beneficial. They showed curiosity about our opinions on certain cases, and we often shared with them how we would handle particular injuries, such as applying ice and heat and teaching the patient exercises. This exchange of ideas was the whole point of the visit.

Intriguing to us, yet unlikely to be absorbed into our own medical ethos, were the traditional compounds and tinctures, many of which have been scientifically analyzed and proven to be effective: dried seahorse for arthritis, dried toad for arthritis and cancer, dried lizard for bronchitis, dried snake for skin rashes, and extract of bamboo for respiratory diseases.

Physical therapy was broken down into four subgroups in China: ultrasound diagnosis, radio frequency therapy for tumors, exercise therapy, and acupuncture. We saw many patients receiving ultrasound, diathermy, exercise instruction, and moxabustion, which was the burning of medicinal herbs on the skin at specific acupuncture points. People climbed into traction harnesses suspended from the ceilings. This self-traction stretched out their backs. Patients also soaked in whirlpool baths containing warm paraffin and herbs to speed up healing.

Anesthesia was almost exclusively done by acupuncture. Depending on the type of surgery, doctors used needles instead of knocking their patients out with expensive drugs. Shockingly enough, it really worked on certain patients!

China had at that time something called the "Barefoot Doctor" program, in which over one million young people, mostly in rural areas, were trained to render basic first aid and care for fevers and coughs. They learned how to set fractures and acted as midwives. Out where the bulk of China's farms were located, there were often no medical facilities except for these "barefoot" clinics. We guessed the term to be merely symbolic of rural life, as the barefoot clinicians we saw wore shoes! This program began under Mao Zedong's regime, because rural communities lacked even the most basic of medical care. These clinics also existed in cities, and we visited the one in Shanghai.

China's methods of healthcare often seemed outdated to us. Or perhaps they were so traditional as to be "cutting edge" by American standards, and we just couldn't yet fathom the benefit of herbs and acupuncture! Either way, the Chinese had made great strides in eradicating certain infectious diseases. Our guides told us that rates of sexually transmitted disease had fallen to an all-time low in the country. They also told us there were no prostitutes in China, but I, for one, did not believe it. If prostitution did not exist officially then it surely existed unofficially!

I did believe, however, that China had succeeded in chasing birds from its territory. Look though I might, I saw very few wild birds sitting in trees or flying across the sky. The absence of birdsong struck me. We did see pet birds in cages, but our guards informed us that because wild birds ate crops and tended to spread disease through their droppings, the country had embarked upon a campaign to frighten them away or kill them by banging pots and pans together, making such a racket that the birds simply left or dropped out of the sky from distress.

When I remarked upon the fact that I saw very few flies anywhere, our guide said, as if it were too obvious to question, "Well, if you give a billion people a fly swatter, eventually, you are going to get rid of all the flies."

The spread of infectious disease loomed large over such densely populated cities as Beijing, Shanghai, and Guangzhou. Thus, litter and trash were picked up immediately. Spitting on the street or sidewalk brought stiff penalties, including jail time, and the streets were washed down every night. The Chinese collected and recycled all waste materials—even human waste, which was used for fertilizer.

At the end of every day, we all ate dinner together in a traditional Chinese restaurant before going to our hotel for the night. Sometimes, Jack and I would go out in the evenings after dinner for a walk. As we strolled through the smoky air, listening to the ever-present tinkling of bicycle bells in the streets, we noticed many people cooking their meals outdoors. They lived in tiny apartments with minimal space for food preparation and no actual kitchens. Many daily activities were performed outside because of this, including haircuts and exercises. Hundreds of people, both old and young, gathered in the early mornings and evenings to do tai chi together. Seeing grandparents teaching their grandchildren how to "sword dance" made us smile. For this activity, they used cardboard or wooden swords by the light of the streetlamps.

We even observed the Chinese people making use of self-physical therapy, so necessary in a country with a huge population and lack of financial resources. Out in the streets, family members, friends, and neighbors gave each other range of motion and did stretching exercises.

It was evident to us that older people played a vital role in their families and communities. In China, the elderly are greatly respected, and those in the countryside often raise their grandchildren when the parents go off to work in cities and live in dormitories. We saw many older people pushing strollers and playing with toddlers outside. With older children, they played ping-pong or card games. These senior citizens formed squads and roamed the neighborhoods, keeping juveniles out of trouble and ensuring crosswalk safety.

One day we visited some factories. From our western perspective, these buildings were poorly lit and therefore made an undesirable work environment. Yet from a health standpoint, the Chinese ethos was progressive in that all the workers were mandated to take exercise breaks every four hours. They might go outside or stay near their desk, machine, or assembly line, but every person was encouraged to stand and follow their supervisor through arm and posture exercises. That was certainly not happening in American factories in 1981! Our idea of a break was for donuts, coffee, or cigarettes. Smoking tobacco in the workplace was highly discouraged in China at that time. Workers drank their beloved tea instead.

Perhaps the highlight of our visit was walking on the Great Wall of China. We happened to be there at a time when national treasures, so long hidden from the eyes of Chinese citizens, were just opening up to them as well as to the handful of foreign tourists starting to trickle in. It was a thrill to see the Forbidden City, from which ordinary people had always had to avert their eyes when passing by. Only royalty and those who served them could see the treasures that lay within. Now we American went traipsing through, admiring the exquisite tile and carvings and works of art, right next to Chinese people whose own parents and grandparents had never been allowed inside. We also saw Chairman Mao lying in state, still well-preserved five years after his death, heavily guarded by armed soldiers. It felt creepy to walk past him!

Whenever we had the chance to speak to people, we heard a similar sentiment: "Before the revolution, my family was starving. We lived in a hut. If someone got sick, they died. Now, I have a home. I can take care of my grandchildren while their parents work. I have rice, and I'm content."

Were these prepared speeches, scripted just for the benefit of us capitalist foreigners? We were not stupid; we knew about Mao's "Great Leap Forward," in the early 1960s, in which around thirty million Chinese people died of starvation under communist mismanagement. But as we looked around us, twenty years after that man-made disaster, many people did seem to have enough to eat and whatever other necessities they required. Life didn't look luxurious, but who were we to say their circumstances hadn't improved? When they praised communism, they seemed sincere. There seemed to be an air of expectation, as if better things were on the horizon. The China we visited in 1981 was indeed on the threshold of change.

Chapter Twenty-One

Brokeback Canyon

On a beautiful but windy April day a little over a decade ago, I stood at the rim of the Grand Canyon with three friends, eager and excited to hike seven miles down to the bottom. This arduous adventure had been planned for a long time. As we laughed, joked, and took photos in preparation to descend, I could not have known that before the day was up, I would change from physical therapist to patient in the most sudden, horrific way.

We'd made our reservations a year in advance, even choosing the meal we would eat at Phantom Ranch at the bottom of the canyon beside the Colorado River. I'd chosen the steak dinner, while some of my friends chose the "hiker's stew." We'd reserved beds in the dorm-like shelter where we planned to spend the night before hiking back out in the morning. As we made our way down the South Kaibab trail, the meal that awaited me grew more and more enticing in my thoughts.

It was the second time for me to hike the Grand Canyon. I'd done it before in my thirties, and now I was in my early sixties. Still healthy and fit, I'd nevertheless taken six months to prepare myself for the rigorous journey by walking up and down hills wearing a heavy backpack. I felt more than capable of finishing out the hike as we made our way downward, "oohing" and "aahing" over all the geological changes visible in the rocks.

This was raw wilderness, with no cell phone reception and no bathrooms with flushing toilets along the trail. Cindy, Denise, Pat, and I had to carry all the water and snacks we needed to fuel our descent to Phantom Ranch. We'd high-fived each other and laughed excitedly at the top of the canyon, but as we hiked downward, we grew more focused, conserving energy to make it safely to the bottom. We enjoyed the hike thoroughly, stopping now and then to take some photos. The wind proved challenging, but at last, we made it!

The floor of the Canyon is desert-like but lush in its own way, with lovely vegetation along the Bright Angel creek and the Colorado River, and huge cottonwood trees that provide longed-for shade. It's warmer down there at the bottom. We'd started out in forty-degree weather at the rim, then found ourselves in a comfortable seventy degrees. After walking for seven hours, we were tired and ready to drink some of the delicious lemonade served at Phantom Ranch, but first we wanted to take off our boots. We sat down on a low rock formation that resembled a wall and began to unlace our footwear. It felt wonderful to sit in the shade of a cottonwood!

I hadn't been there for more than five minutes when I felt a breeze kick up. A strong gust of wind swept through the canyon. That's when a dead limb, twelve feet up on a cottonwood tree, snapped loose. It hurled through the air and slammed into my back. The next thing I knew, I was face down, flattened in the dirt, the limb lying on top of me. It had missed my friends and singled me out with near-deadly force. I felt a sharp pain and screamed, "Help!"

Pat immediately got down in the dirt with me. "We're here, Martha," she said, trying to keep me calm. "It's going to be OK." While Denise ran for help, Cindy, in a rush of adrenaline, heaved the heavy limb off my back with an "Ummph!" My shoulder and back hurt terribly. Denise came running back with two young rangers. One of them, examining and trying to lift the limb that had fallen, exclaimed, "Damn, that's heavy!" He looked at Cindy, marveling at the fact that such a small woman had been able to lift it.

Assessing me as best they could, the rangers asked where it hurt, and if I could wiggle my toes. To my great relief, I could. One man stayed with me while the other ran back to the little ranger station. He returned with an eccentric canyon-dweller named Walt, who often volunteered to help the rangers; they carried a backboard because they didn't know the extent of my injuries. Gently they rolled me onto it and strapped me down. By now, I had an audience. Curious hikers gathered around to watch the proceedings, wondering what had happened to put me in this unenviable position. When they found out about the freak accident, their eyes wandered suspiciously up to the cottonwood trees, warily watching the branches swaying in the wind.

The rangers looked me over as best they could, although they were not paramedics. By now it was 5:00 p.m.—too late for a helicopter to evacuate me that night, but they ordered one for the next morning.

I'd already been having back problems due to falling out of a hammock and the nature of my work, which meant lifting heavy patients on a daily basis. A chiropractor had done some high-velocity manipulations on me, causing more problems. I'd been recovering nicely from all those issues and was now able to work again, but I knew this incident would set me back. As I lay immobile in the ranger station, I couldn't help but wonder, as a widow who needed to support myself, *What's going to become of me now?*

I was filthy dirty from the hike, and also from lying in the dirt. Dust, leaves, and twigs clung to my hair. The rangers treated me kindly, and Walt, the volunteer who preferred life in a canyon where the only way he could obtain groceries was to hike seven miles uphill or ride a mule for twelve hours, stayed by my side and attended to my needs. Pat stayed with me too. I was now lying on a firm table, which was exactly what I needed.

The rangers strongly advised me to allow myself to be taken by ambulance to Flagstaff Medical Center once the helicopter got me to the rim of the canyon. I refused. Not wanting a bumpy, two-hour ambulance ride, I thought I knew best and told them I preferred to go to the small clinic at the rim.

"You should rethink that," said the rangers.

Again, I refused. I wasn't thinking clearly. Crazily, I focused on finances, thinking an ambulance ride would set me back financially, and also worrying that I knew absolutely no one in Flagstaff and would feel isolated there. In hindsight, this was all foolishness, but I remained stubborn. "If someone can get me some crutches," I insisted, "I can make it to the clinic and have an X-ray."

That night, a generous young ranger gave me his bed to sleep in while he bedded down in a tent outdoors. I loaded up on Tylenol and Ibuprofen and Walt rigged up a way for me to drink from a tube leading to a bag of water suspended from an IV pole. In his fifties, Walt was slim and trim from hiking in and out of the canyon. Deeply tanned from constant exposure to the sun, he was far from being a loner-type, conversing chattily and putting me at ease. Pat brought me some hiker's stew—consisting of boiled beef, potatoes, and carrots—because there were no steak dinners left. Oh, how I'd looked forward to that steak! Before I settled in for that long, uncomfortable night, I managed to get to the bathroom with Pat's help and the crutches.

The next morning, when they learned that I was still clinging to my stubborn opinions about what was best for me, the rangers made me sign a release form stating I was going against their recommendations by refusing to take the ambulance to Flagstaff. They loaded me into a helicopter, and I waved goodbye to my hiking buddies. Soon enough, I arrived at the rim of the canyon. The doctor at the small clinic asked me where I was having most of my pain, and I told him my shoulder blade was hurting the most. For that reason, he x-rayed my upper back but not my lower back. Because I could bend and straighten my knees, he told me he thought everything was fine, and he gave me a prescription for a muscle relaxant and pain pills and told me to stay in bed and ice the affected areas.

I stayed in bed at a hotel, in serious pain, until my friends hiked out and joined me the following day. They were extremely attentive to me, and they drove me home to Scottsdale—a journey I could only make thanks to strong pain medication. Cindy, Pat, and Denise unloaded me at my house and said goodbye. They all thought I was doing just fine because I was walking around on crutches. But after a few days of intense pain, I decided to call an orthopedic surgeon. His office staff insisted they could not get me in until the following week, no matter how much I insisted I'd had a terrible accident and needed immediate help.

My eyes were now open, and I was thinking much more clearly about my condition. I knew I'd made a big mistake in not following the rangers' advice. Had I gone to Flagstaff, they would have x-rayed my entire back, put me in a brace, and immediately sent me to an orthopedist. Now, I was stuck, having to wait for help for an injury I suspected was far more serious than I'd imagined. Rather than diminishing, my pain increased with each passing day.

When I finally got in to see the doctor and he saw the nature of my injury, he apologized that his staff had failed to get me in sooner. He ordered full spinal X-rays, which revealed a fracture of L1. "Well, you're here *now*," he said, "and the first thing I'm going to do is order a rigid brace for you." I should have had that rigid brace immediately, he said. I'd been moving around far too much for someone with such severe back trauma.

The brace helped tremendously. The stability it gave reduced my pain and gave me confidence that I was on the road to healing. When an injured back is not rigidly supported, a person can accidentally twist or bend too far, exacerbating the problem or even causing further damage. The brace was exactly what I needed to start feeling better! And although the doctor was irritated with his staff for not getting me in sooner, I knew I really had no one but myself to blame for the delay in treatment.

A few weeks later, as the fracture began its long process of healing, I asked the doctor if I could go up to my cabin in Munds Park to recover. He told me to wait a week, and then if I promised to walk using two hiking poles and wear my brace at all times, he would release me to go. So, that's what I did. I had no desire to stay in Phoenix where it was hotter than Hades. My friends drove up to visit me in Munds Park. I even developed a new hobby as I recovered. Because I spent so much time lying on a cot on my front porch, observing all the fascinating things going on in my yard, I discovered a whole new world out there of birds and plants and insects, simply because I could do nothing else! I became a serious bird watcher, and I still enjoy that hobby today.

Never in my wildest dreams as a therapist had I imagined I would ever become a patient. We "save the world," helper types rarely do! But now I gained another perspective. I learned what it meant to be a patient versus a caregiver. To walk with a heavy back brace and hiking poles and have people come up to me and ask me what was wrong. Even though I'd taken care of many elderly women with fractured spines due to osteoporosis, I'd never fully understood the intensity of their pain. Now, finally, I could empathize with them. At last, I understood the frustration of the disabled, who could not simply jump in a car and drive wherever they wanted to go. I depended upon my friends to bring me groceries.

For the first six months, I oversaw my own physical therapy. But when the orthopedist reassessed me that October, he sent me to outpatient therapy, because I needed it despite the fact that I was feeling much better. How weird it felt to be the patient!

After the accident, I went back to work only ten hours a week, until the very physical tasks of physical therapy began to put too much strain on my back. At that point, I left my beloved profession and went into teaching at Gateway Community College. Instructing first year nursing students and PT assistants felt worthwhile to me and I enjoyed it, although it could never replace the thrill of physically placing hands on patients and guiding them toward healing. I taught some basic core classes until I retired.

By then, a whole new world had begun to open up to me—a world with which I'd had little contact in my privileged life, and which was about to touch me deeply in a whole new way.

Chapter Twenty-Two

Serving on the South Side

After I became semi-retired, a longtime friend and co-worker named Denise presented me with a suggestion that intrigued me. As a member of a local Catholic church, she had become acquainted with Sister Adele O'Sullivan, a nun and physician who had begun a medical clinic for homeless and underserved people in South Phoenix. The idea of volunteering there appealed to Denise, and she wondered if I would like to join her for just one-half day per week. I had free time at my disposal, so I said I would do it.

When Denise and I first pulled into the parking lot of the Healthcare for the Homeless Clinic on the southern side of downtown Phoenix, just off where Washington and Seventh Avenue come together, I shuddered and had to take a deep breath to steady myself. I was right in the middle of a blighted part of town I had always avoided. The clinic had been built in a deplorable setting. The building itself was clean and nice, but the surrounding area was devoid of vegetation. Dry, dusty, and unpleasant, the neighborhood was filled with homeless people, many of whose lives were characterized by substance abuse or mental illness. On one side of us lay an old graveyard. On the other side were some railroad tracks and a mountain of car tires. Years of living in green, well-manicured Scottsdale had not prepared me for this harsher reality of the Phoenix area.

Sister Adele, a member of the Sisters of St. Joseph of Carondelet community, had founded the Circle the City Foundation to care for vulnerable people who had few options in life. Her clinic was part of a larger entity called the Human Services Campus that included a homeless shelter, a dentist's office, and offices where people could sign up for government services like social security and help finding jobs. Nearby stood a Catholic soup kitchen called André's.

Upon meeting Sister Adele, I was impressed by her unassuming, yet cheerful presence. As the small, bespectacled woman walked around the clinic dressed in casual clothes with a stethoscope around her neck, she radiated compassion and kindness to all she encountered. She had surrounded herself with a small but excellent staff consisting of nurses, physician's assistants, and social workers.

The clinic impressed me too. Homeless and underserved people could come in off the street, take a seat in the huge, air-conditioned waiting room, and be seen by a provider for free. That desolate part of town had become a hive of humanitarian activity that made a huge difference in people's lives. In the tiny room designated for physical therapy, Denise and I set to work. Sister Adele herself brought us our patients.

"Martha, this is Janet," she would say with a friendly smile. "She's having trouble with her back. Or she would say, "Denise, meet John. His neck is hurting."

People who live on the streets are brutalized by their environment. Exposed to the harsh and unrelenting rays of the sun, they walk around day and night. Their joints are overused. Their legs get worn out. There wasn't a lot we could do for them except give them the comfort of massages, and we evaluated them for whether they needed better shoes from the well-stocked donation closet at the clinic. We also had backpacks, socks, underwear, and jackets to give out to those who most needed them. It always felt so rewarding to me to rummage around the closet and return to a patient with a new pair of shoes, because it made them so happy.

Most of our patients were unhoused, but some of them were merely those who had a roof over their heads but no health insurance. Serving them became the most rewarding chapter of my entire career. Even though I dreaded driving down into that ugly environment each week, I knew that the small things we did to help made a huge impact on these people's lives. Just having someone pay attention to them, listening to their troubles, and hearing all about their aches and pains, provided great comfort.

Of course, we did our best to address their specific issues with our limited means. We showed them exercises and gave them a cane if they needed one. Some of them could barely walk because of injuries, and we had a whole closet filled with canes and walkers. These were individuals who did not have the resources to simply walk into Walgreens and buy a cane.

We gave people ultrasound treatments for sore muscles. We placed hot packs on the places that hurt. They loved it! Especially during the winter months when it was chilly, those hot packs provided tremendous relief. As often as I could, I would put a hot pack on someone's back and turn out the lights, saying, "You can take a little thirty-minute nap." For someone pounding the pavement day and night, this was a huge blessing.

I felt honored to be part of this outreach, and to this day, I have tremendous respect for the City of Phoenix and what it has done. Perhaps some of the most poignant cases I saw were migrants from south of the border. They were always incredibly thankful for our services! The privilege of seeing a doctor, finding out they were diabetic and receiving medication, or even just getting a new pair of shoes, overwhelmed them with gratitude.

One man, who may have only been in his forties but looked as if he were in his late fifties, had black hair with a few strands of gray just beginning to appear. Juan was short and sinewy, without an ounce of fat on him. His weather-beaten skin had darkened drastically from the sun. He was having trouble with his knees, and he needed shoes and socks. We soaked his feet and put hot packs on his knees to give him some relief, and as we did so, little by little, Juan's story spilled

216

out through a Spanish interpreter. He said, "My feet hurt because I walked here from Guatemala."

Juan hadn't seen a doctor for ten years, because medical care was not available anywhere near his home village. For part of Juan's northward journey, he'd jumped on the train known as The Beast, or *El Bestia*, that runs through Mexico. He talked about migrants riding on top of that train, sometimes falling asleep and falling off in the night. Some of Juan's friends had been killed in this way. Some of them didn't know how to jump on the moving train correctly. These unfortunate ones lost arms or legs in the resulting accidents. Juan had left his whole family behind in Guatemala, and he dreamed of doing any kind of work he could find so he could send money home to them. Violent gangs had driven him out of his home country, and he hated to leave his loved ones behind in that frightening atmosphere, but felt he had no choice.

This dear man treasured the tennis shoes, T-shirt, sweatshirt, and socks we gave him. As did so many others in his circumstances, he'd been wearing flimsy flip-flops and whatever else he could find after wearing out his clothes on the long, northward trek. Juan ended up being our patient for quite some time because he had severe health issues like high blood pressure and diabetes. For these conditions, we saw him twice a month.

What Denise and I did for these patients wasn't much more than icing on a cake. Yet, Sister Adele and the nurses could only spend so much time with people. That's why our listening ears and therapeutic touch were so important for their emotional well-being. We had a little more time to spend with them, and the things we did brought comfort. With time, I also felt moved to bring encouragement to the staff in the way of art. One day, I looked around the clinic and realized that although it was spick and span, it had bare walls devoid of beauty. After asking permission, I bought large photographic posters of gorgeous Arizona scenery such as the mountains, forests, and deserts in bloom. I framed them and hung them around the clinic, knowing it would lift the spirits of the staff as well as the patients.

We saw a great variety of people, all from widely varying backgrounds. Some were young mothers with children, living in low-income housing. They had no health insurance. Some resided in women's shelters because they had fled domestic violence at home. Some women were prostitutes.

Like Juan, the other men who came from Guatemala or

Honduras or parts of Mexico seemed content and happy despite

their dire circumstances. They felt they had so much in this

country that they never could have hoped for in their former

countries. To them, America truly was a land of milk and

honey. If they were lucky, they had a cot to sleep on in the

homeless shelter at night. The fact that their basic needs were

being met put smiles on their faces. They often said things like,

"God is good!" and "I thank God every day that I found this

place."

Over, and over again, we heard the Spanish phrase,

"*Mucho dolor.*" Much pain.

On Tuesday mornings, when Denise and I finished our

work, hopped in the hot car, and drove back to Scottsdale, we

watched the scenery gradually change. The farther east we

drove, the more vegetation began to appear, and the houses got

bigger. Expensive cars moved along the road beside us. We

began to see more flowers and parks. I noticed people in

spandex, biking or walking on well-manicured trails, gold or

diamond jewelry flashing from women's ears, necks, and

fingers. We made a habit of going out to lunch on Tuesdays after working at the clinic, just to celebrate that we had made it through the morning. Yet our attitude wasn't one of disgust, but contentment over a job well done.

One lovely spring day when Denise could not accompany me to the clinic, I drove down by myself, car windows open to let in the refreshing breeze. As I pulled off Washington Avenue to turn into the clinic property, I saw a police officer down on one knee, pointing a gun with two hands and shouting at a man to drop his weapon. "Lay down in the dirt!" he commanded.

What the heck is going on? I wondered as I managed to get into the parking lot and stop the car. Inside the clinic, the grieving staff told me that a shelter worker they knew and liked had become involved in an altercation and been shot and killed. Everyone was crying. They closed down the clinic and refused to see any patients for the rest of the day. I had driven right past the perpetrator as the police apprehended him.

This type of drama was not unusual in that neighborhood. The clinic was located in a high-crime area. People wandered around, standing on corners, clutching sleeping bags or plastic bags filled with their belongings. Wandering aimlessly, many of them were drunk or high on drugs. Mentally ill people shuffled around, talking to themselves. Plenty of good Samaritans did selfless work in this area, handing out water, picking people up in vans to take them to medical services. But overall, it was a scary place, and most of Phoenix's citizens avoided it.

Sister Adele's work expanded. Closer to downtown on Indian School Road, she added a small inpatient clinic with ten beds, where people who needed it could receive more comprehensive care. For that new facility, Denise and I were allowed to design and order equipment for a PT room. It wasn't fancy. It had a mat table, hand weights, ice packs, and hot packs. Just the basics. Yet, we felt privileged to have a part in outfitting such a necessary component of the new clinic's ministry. We began volunteering there too.

Many of the people we saw in that new clinic had been kicked out of the hospital with no place to go. They'd been dropped off on the curb and somehow made their way to us. If we had room, we admitted them.

In my opinion, Sister Adele is the Mother Teresa of Phoenix, although she is far too humble to allow herself that comparison. A petite dynamo, she modeled tirelessness in service to those less fortunate than her and inspired so many of us to reach out and serve alongside her. I felt privileged to be involved with her ministry to the homeless and underserved. Adele made sure her clinics had an atmosphere of peace about them. At the inpatient clinic, I used to go into the chapel at the end of my shift for a short communion service. That comforted me. The good work being done by Circle the City taught me gratitude and humility. It gave me a perspective I would never otherwise have had, and it fulfilled me in a way that my regular PT career never could.

Chapter Twenty-Three

The Lure of Walmart

One Sunday, a retired Methodist pastor visited the church I attended and presented his ministry called Faith Works—a medical mission that served Mexican citizens in Agua Prieta, just across the border from Douglas, Arizona. With a name that meant "brown water," Agua Prieta was far from being a tourist destination, but the thought of going there to help people enticed me. I was retired and had time on my hands. I'd had such a good experience volunteering with Circle the City in Phoenix that I felt hungry to contribute again. I listened raptly to the pastor describe how he took volunteer teams across the border three times a year, running a medical clinic to serve the poorer neighborhoods of the Mexican town.

His speech was so inspirational! After the service, I approached him and asked if he could use the help of a licensed physical therapist. He said he most certainly could. For some reason, I'd always assumed missionaries had to travel to faraway places like Africa, but now, for the first time, I realized I could do mission work relatively close to home. I couldn't wait!

I already knew Linda, one of the retired nurses who'd volunteered with Faith Works, so I connected with her and signed up. When the time came, I packed a few necessities and hopped in a van along with eight other volunteers for the drive down to the border. The van was loaded down with supplies: Tylenol, Advil, bandages—all the basics. We took plenty of bottled water. Our goal was not to supply medicine for major diseases like high blood pressure or diabetes, but to do such simple things as eye exams and handing out over-the-counter medication to people who had nothing. Our patients would be farm laborers and employees of a mini-blind factory, people who were paid next to nothing for a hard day's labor. These inhabitants of the poorer areas of Agua Prieta had sparse access to even the most basic of medical care.

We checked into our rooms at Motel Six in Douglas, a drab building with a prison adjacent to it. Our food was to be equally unglamorous. We mostly planned to eat pizza or fast food in the evenings after long days of working. Our leader thought that since our purpose was to serve people, we had no business living in luxury. I had to agree. We only needed food for fuel, and we would not be spending time at the motel except to sleep. The bulk of our time would be spent over the border, from early morning until late in the evening. This schedule was a challenge for me! As a night owl who seldom went to bed before midnight, I knew I had to get my butt down to the parking lot by 6:30 a.m. to get in the van for our drive into Mexico.

The first time we drove across the border, I got a good look at the wall that separated the United States and Mexico. It loomed tall, intimidating, and imposing. On that first day, I had no idea just how prominent that wall figured in the lives of the people we would be treating.

We set up our clinic in a simple concrete block building with a bathroom inside. By 8:00 a.m. on that first morning and on each following morning, over 100 people—mothers, babies, children, women, and men of all ages—had lined up, eager to be seen. We got everything ready and opened our doors. As other volunteers prepared to give eye exams and dispense medication, I scanned the crowd and thought, *What the heck am I going to do here today?*

As it turned out, I did plenty. The other volunteers sent a steady stream of people to me, each one complaining of "*Mucho dolor!*" Many women in Agua Prieta earned a living by making tortillas and walking around the streets to sell them. "I make tortillas all day," they explained through an interpreter. "My hands are sore; my arms are sore; my neck is sore." I could do little for them but massage their aching muscles, using therapeutic touch, putting into practice a common saying among physical therapists: *If it's physical, it's therapy*. When I laid hands on these women, they felt heard, seen, and comforted.

By lunchtime, I was so exhausted that I sat down, laid my head on the table, and slept soundly.

One young man name Eduardo came to us in a wheelchair, pushed by his mother Francisca. Francisca looked more like his sister and was probably only about sixteen years older than her son. Like most other teenage boys in the area, Eduardo had dreamed of making his way over the border and getting a job at the Walmart in Douglas. That store dazzled the young people of Agua Prieta—so close, and yet so far! Temptation nagged Eduardo, egging him on to climb the wall.

Finally, he'd succumbed, but as he attempted the climb, he lost his grip, fell off, and landed on his head. Now in his early twenties, he was mostly paralyzed on one side of his body, with only minimal use of his right arm and leg. He couldn't walk; he had a slight speech deficit. I knew that Eduardo would never be able to work unless his body had some kind of spontaneous recovery, and I couldn't help but think that if he'd had access to decent medical care after his fall, he might have had a chance.

I exercised Eduardo's arm and leg and did range of motion. Terribly thin, he'd lost muscle mass from spending so much time sitting in the wheelchair. His neck hurt, so I applied microwavable hot packs to it. This gave him relief. I showed Francisca how to strengthen his arm and leg by doing exercises with him. With his mother helping and with an interpreter in the room to relay my instructions, I got Eduardo to take a few steps. His balance wasn't good, but I gave him a cane and using it, he was able to do better.

Through the interpreter, Eduardo managed to tell me with his limited speech that no decent jobs existed for young men like him in Agua Prieta. The American-owned mini-blind factory paid only a pittance for a long, hard day's work. If one didn't work there or do farm work, there was little chance of earning even a partial living. Many of his friends had managed to successfully scale the wall and find jobs in America.

I knew Eduardo had probably suffered a brain bleed from his fall, and I hoped that with time, if the swelling went down, he might regain some function. He was so young that his body just might be able to fight back. But it can take a very long time for brain swelling to recede.

Eduardo's story broke my heart. He was young and handsome, with his whole life ahead of him. All he'd wanted to do was escape grinding poverty, and I couldn't fault him for that. He was understandably depressed and listless. His young mother, her long ponytail still with no hint of gray, dressed in jeans and a sweatshirt to ward off the November chill, had her hands full taking care of a son who should have been in the full bloom of life and able to ease her financial burden by working. Now, out of necessity, Francisca had joined the other women in making tortillas and pounding the pavement to sell them.

Chapter Twenty-Four

Cabbage Knees

"Mucho dolor. Mucho dolor."

When I put my hands on Diego's knees, I could feel the crepitus—bony spurs that cracked and popped whenever he bent and straightened his leg. This condition was hardly surprising, given that Diego spent all day on his knees, picking cabbage in a field in cold weather. Northern Mexico's higher altitude meant that when Diego and his fellow farm workers began their shift at 5 a.m., freezing temperatures could chill them to the bone. Kneeling in cold dirt will do nobody's knees any good.

I put Diego on the table and applied hot packs to his knees. I massaged them. I showed him some simple strengthening exercises and admonished him to repeat them three times a day. "Take breaks from your work throughout the day," I said, although I had no idea whether he was even allowed to do so.

Diego looked to be in his mid-forties, and like most of the men I encountered in Mexico, he was small of stature and sinewy, his muscles taut from hard work. He appeared happy to be at the clinic where someone could pay attention to his physical complaints. Everyone who came to the clinic was so grateful to be there! I sensed a strong community spirit among them; they all knew each other and looked out for each other. They possessed so little yet had so much in the way of friendship and belonging.

Although Diego told me he was in constant pain, all I could do was give him Advil and Tylenol. Those medications would help to get him through the day, I knew, but I also understood that there would come a time when the pain became so great that he would no longer be able to work. What then?

As my teammates and I walked around Agua Prieta's dirt roads, we saw people living in the open, sleeping under bushes, camping in the dirt. These were not immigrants from Central America hoping to cross the border, but Mexican citizens and residents of the town. Our team leader said the living conditions there rivaled those he had seen in the poorest parts of Africa. We passed tiny hovels with earthen floors and lean-to dwellings made of plywood and corrugated tin. People used ditches behind their homes as toilets. Electricity was spotty, coming on and going off seemingly at will throughout the day. It boggled my mind that all this existed within a stone's throw of the American border. On the other side lay Douglas, Arizona, with its modern plumbing, air-conditioned restaurants and stores, and a big-chain drugstore stocked with medication. On the other side, opportunity awaited—opportunity worth risking one's precious life for. Douglas seemed as magical and elusive to the people of Agua Prieta as the Emerald City of Oz.

The citizens of Agua Prieta's low-income neighborhoods were desperate. They had nothing. It felt so good to give them even our limited supplies of over-the-counter medications and, more importantly, our time and attention. An elderly woman came to every clinic, year after year. She enjoyed having someone look at her, *really* see her, and take her complaints seriously. People brought their small children, knowing that one of our team members would occupy them in the clinic's play area long enough to allow their weary parents to receive some medical attention.

Each morning before we started work, we stood in a prayer circle and listened to a short devotional. Sometimes, it made me cry. I could feel my heart breaking for so many of the people who walked in to be seen by us. One older lady came to every single clinic run by Faith Works, year after year. She had no teeth, and she showed up scantily dressed. Through the interpreter, she told me she had many children, but she never saw them. Knowing the Mexican nights could be extremely cold, I gave her my coat. Later, our leader said to me, "We can't be giving people our coats or clothing, Martha. We don't have enough for everyone." I understood that completely. The woman's clouded eyes and toothless smile had gotten to me, and I realized that I was probably not the only one who had handed her a coat over the years. I knew then that if I continued to come to Agua Prieta with Faith Works, I was going to have to develop thicker skin and keep a tighter rein on my emotions.

I marveled at the great number of teen pregnancies in Agua Prieta. These young girls seemed happy and content, proudly showing off their protruding bellies and their infants. With no education or career on the horizon, having a baby was a sign of prestige among them, whether or not they had the means to support the child. Our interpreter explained that school wasn't really an option for many girls, because although public schools were free, students couldn't attend unless they could buy uniforms, books, and supplies. Cultural mores strongly encouraged the men to work in fields or the mini-blind factory and the women to raise children at home, so it felt natural for a young woman to value becoming a mother—the sooner the better. Making and selling tortillas on the side gave women, both young and old, a bit extra to help make ends meet.

Like Eduardo's mother, Francisca, many of these young women dealt with severely disabled children in the home. As in America, cerebral palsy was the most common cause of childhood disabilities, but resources were extremely limited if not non-existent. Agua Prieta had no children's clinic that we knew of, although there may have been one within reach for those with wealth. We only saw the poorest of the poor.

One day, the women in the community put their resources together and served us a delicious lunch with homemade tortillas and tamales. The chicken dish and soup they cooked for us were fabulous! They beamed with pride as they dished out the food, and we realized it was their way of giving back. Likewise, the Methodist church service held in our honor was their way of thanking us. This church was doing its best to get the message out to young people that there was a better way to deal with grinding poverty than drugs and drinking.

The young members of the congregation danced, sang, and played guitars and drums for us. It was beautiful! Their warmth and emotional expression in worship touched my heart and thawed this member of the "frozen chosen," who had been raised in a stiff and formal Presbyterian church environment. Jumping and jiving, the young people gave us hugs and thanked us profusely for leaving our families to come and help their community.

My time in Agua Prieta was a rich and rewarding experience—so much so that I came back several more times and brought my friend Denise along. It seemed only right to introduce her to the work in Mexico, because she had introduced me to Circle the City's ministry in Phoenix. I had the chance to "pay it forward." When I had to stop going to Agua Prieta because of back problems, Denise and her husband continued going several more times.

More Than a Career

In my nearly forty-year career as a physical therapist, I learned that three things will make a difference in how well a person recovers after a severe or devastating injury or illness:

1. Attitude

You can't change what happened to you, but you can change your attitude about it. Those patients who are able to keep a sense of humor and set goals do best. A "poor me" attitude just drags one down. There will always be someone who is much worse off than you. Staying positive in one's outlook means everything.

2. A good fitness level prior to your injury or surgery.

Maintaining your fitness at every stage of life is a must. We have to keep moving and stay as fit and strong as we can. Those patients I cared for who did not stay fit did not respond well to their injuries. Being already weak and out of shape put them in a precarious situation. Some people just cannot recover from an injury or surgery if they are already debilitated.

3. A good support system of friends and family

We all need to have a cheer team as we recover from illness or injury. Recovery can't be done well if a person is alone. The patients I cared for that recovered the best had caring people in their lives. Visits and phone calls from friends or family mean everything to an injured person. Having someone to cheer you on with encouragement is extremely important to a recovering person.

Over my years as a physical therapist, whether earning money or volunteering, whether practicing my profession in the United States or over the border, encountering and helping patients who were in the midst of experiencing the worst days of their lives grew empathy in me. Often, my heart broke wide open as I listened to stories of suffering, both mental and physical. Helping these people get better by inches taught me patience. Incredibly impressive to me was the courage of people who were facing severe limitations from catastrophic injuries. I often wondered, *What would I do in their shoes?*

To this day, when I notice a person who is paralyzed in any way, whether from stroke or accident, it can bring me to tears. I know the struggles they face on a daily basis. I would not trade this "knowing" for anything, for through it, I enter into the larger human experience. Such people are often shut away from us, and we can go through life not having to see or think about those who live with drastically limited mobility. May our eyes and hearts be opened to see, to understand, and to contribute to healing however we can.

Left to right: Ada Boesch, Martha Thomas, Maxine

Thomas